A Woodcarver's Primer

by John Upton

Drake Publishers Inc. New York

Published in 1976 by
Drake Publishers Inc.
801 Second Ave.
New York, N.Y. 10017

Library of Congress Cataloging in Publication Data

Upton, John, 1897-
     A woodcarver's primer.

     1. Wood-carving.   I. Title.
TT199.7.U67   736'.4   73-4345
ISBN 0-87749-494-0

Printed in The United States of America

Table Of Contents

Foreword

The practice of woodcarving is a one man proposition. It is an art for the loner, the man who wishes to work for himself and make the things he wants to make, hopeful that in so doing he can earn a living as well.

More than a century ago this trade, for that is really what it is, commercially, was practiced in a number of different shops, such as those making fine furniture, picture frames, shops where ecclesiastical furniture and other religious objects were made, and in shipyards. These fields are for the most part extinct. Carvings are now made by machines in sets of dozens and sold at give-away prices. Sometimes not so give-away, too.

The loner can work up a satisfactory business if he has an imagination, a love of hard work and all the patience in the world to learn the mastery of the trade. Otherwise, he can starve amidst the plenty.

So far as I know, this art is not taught in art schools as an ''art.'' You can take courses in sculpture, using inert clays and metals as the medium of expression and occasionally learn something about wood, but not as a finished course. The trade, or art if you must doll the business up in fine feathers, has to be more or less learned by yourself—from short works such as this book, and by taking lessons from a patient man. That is, if you can find someone who can teach and who is willing to do so.

Fig. 1–1 Carved panels done in black walnut represent-ing the sacrament, the bread, and the wine. They are in the Chapel of the Heavenly Rest, Springfield, Ohio. Gift of Lee Bayley.

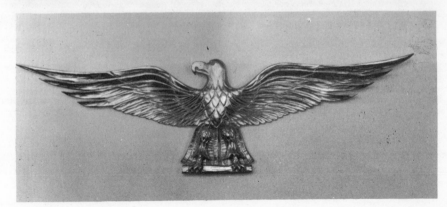

Fig. 1–2 Broad eagle carved and gilded in pine—42" wingspread, 15" tall, 2" thick.

Opposite page: Bottom left, Fig. 1–3 Golden pheasant made in Honduras mahogany, linseed oil finish. Right, top to bottom, Fig. 1–4 Great horned owl carved alto relievo in cherry. Fig. 1–5 Girandole carved in mahogany and gilded, one of a pair—19 1/2" wide, 37" tall, about 1 3/4" thick. Fig. 1–6 Puffin carved in pine and polychromed.

1

A Woodcarver's Primer

Woodcarving is the art of taking away all the wood on a piece of stock that does not belong on the finished piece.

In selecting the material from which a carving is made, I think the following woods can be used to great advantage:

Honduras Mahogany, which is a moderately hard wood but very workable under the knife. It is reddish brown in color, usually available at good hardwood dealers.

Native northern white pine is a soft whitish wood with an even grain structure, also easily carved and is usually available in clear stock.

Black walnut is a hard dense wood, readily cut with properly sharpened tools and is available at most hardwood dealer's yards. Its color is very dark brown, almost black.

Native white oak is a dense wide grained hardwood also readily cut with properly sharpened and shaped tools and is commonly available in reasonable dimension. Its use is for the most part limited to church work.

Teak is a dense hardwood, the grain is strongly marked and when carved makes a beautiful finished piece and for which no further finish need be applied. It, too, is readily available and is one of the finest woods for use by a woodcarver who can take the trouble to keep his tools sharp.

There are other woods less commonly used and most of them, in my opinion, are not worth spending time on because of the lack of good carving characteristics. They are African mahogany, Philippine mahogany, tupelo, white wood, and a host of others.

The important thing to keep in mind is that some woods lend themselves to fine detail work, such as Honduras mahogany and black walnut. Pine and oak are more brittle and less easily detailed. Teak is better used for the bolder pieces.

2
The
Workshop

It is essential that the workbench on which you propose to do your carving be firmly fixed to the floor, and that there is room about it so you can work freely without being restricted in your movements.

Light from artificial sources is best placed overhead near or at the center of the bench space. Daylight should come from windows at one side and one end of the bench as well; this will avoid hard shadows.

A wall bench or table close at hand on which your tools may be placed is a convenience. Other shelves for the storage of the sundries, like glue, hardware, that is nails, brads and wood screws, your sharpening stones and the hundred other bits of clutter you gather are also needed.

Proper care and storage for your carving tools is necessary. A tightly covered tin can of some sort for the storage of oily papers and rags is an absolute necessity if you are to avoid fire. Heat from an adequate stove or heater of some sort is also important, and a wastebasket in one corner in which the daily sweepings from the floor can be put is a convenience as well. Keep the floor clear of chips and sawdust as a safety factor.

Be sure you have adequate workspace around the mechanical tools and that they are firmly mounted on suitable stands. All electric wiring should be installed so there is no danger of cutting or scraping off the insulation as work progresses on the table extensions for the power tools.

A tackboard on which your hand tools of many sorts can be hung for quick access is valuable if you have the wall space available. The tackboard in my shop is shown. Fig. 2–1

Fig. 2–1 Tack board and hand tools usually used.

*Fig 2–2 Workbench and
carving frame
—top, 38" x 36";
height, 37" from top to floor.
Note woodworking vise.*

The top of your carving frame must be at a proper and comfortable distance from the floor. If it is too high, you will get cramped—too low and you will get tired of stooping over. You will find it convenient to have a woodworker's vise put on one side of the carving frame. This, too, is pictured. Fig. 2–2

Adequate ventilation is a must. Do not work in a tightly closed up shop when you use these modern "mucks" the chemists have conjured up. If the container says the fumes may be dangerous, the chances are somebody found that out the hard way and no longer has any concern.

You may think you are a real toughy—you are no such thing.

Learn the routine care of all your power and hand tools. Be sure you know how to put an edge on your carving tools and how to keep them clean and free from gums and nicks.

Have a place for everything and see to it everything is in its proper place. This will save time, temper and ulcers.

If you are in the habit of lending your toothbrush to some person, you are at liberty to lend your carving tools, likewise; otherwise, don't.

3
Power Tools
for the Workshop

It is not necessary to load your shop up with a lot of power-operated, mechanical "monsters."

I have three of these items in my shop I use most of the time and a turning lathe used very occasionally. The three tools most commonly used are these: a bench-mounted bandsaw, six-inch capacity; a rotary saw and table; and a drill press, also bench-mounted. Figs. 3–1, 3–2, and 3–3

Above left, Fig. 3–1 Bandsaw. Note the limited size of its table. Above right, Fig. 3–2 Rotary saw and movable table. Motor mounted under guard in rear. Right: Fig. 3–3 Bench mounted drill press. Note limited size of its table.

I find that three portable power tools are a great help. Mine consist of an orbital sanding device, a hand-held power drill, quarter-inch capacity chuck and a sabresaw for inside and outside cutting on large awkward pieces.

I use high speed steel fractional drills for most of my boring jobs; carbon steel drills lose their edge too soon in wood.

I do not have and will not have that finger-clipper called a planer-jointer. It is a lethal tool at best.

One shop tip here is most pertinent. Do not wear loose, floppy clothing in the shop; dangling ends and tatters can foul you up in the machines.

There will be times when the size of the piece on which work is to be done is too big to be easily held and manipulated on the small table top with which the bandsaw and the drill press are fitted. Extension tops for these tools are easily made out of ³/₄" plywood. These extensions are shown in Figs. 3–4 and 3–5.

After many years of work on the rotary saw, I find that if the tool and motor are mounted on a table that can be readily moved about the shop floor, the value of this "monster" is greatly increased and its use practically unlimited.

Left, Fig. 3–4 Bandsaw fitted with extension top of 3/4" plywood. Right, Fig. 3–5 Drill press with extension top made of 3/4" plywood.

4
Hand Tools

You supposedly will have the usual collection of handyman tools on hand, such as hammers, planes, saws, screwdrivers, a bittstock and some bitts, perhaps an egg-beater hand drill and a few broken down drills of odd sizes. Most of us have such a collection lying about somewhere.

To start woodcarving, you will need specially shaped tools of various sorts and sizes. These carving tools are readily available from dealers and other specialty houses handling such things. These tools are available in comprehensive sets of a dozen or so and the sets have been made up as a result of some considerable experience in selling the various sorts to many people. I suggest you invest in such a set to start with.

In addition to the tools, you will need various sharpening stones of different kinds. An oil stone with a coarse and a fine face, properly boxed is a must, likewise the slips which are used to put the fine edge on the variously shaped carving tools. A hone stone and a strop are valuable assets to sharp tools.

I see no need to go all out to begin with in buying all the many kinds of tools temptingly set forth in the usual catalogues. Why buy tools you will use once or twice a year? Make do with what you have.

Don't forget to buy a round mallet of suitable weight and size.

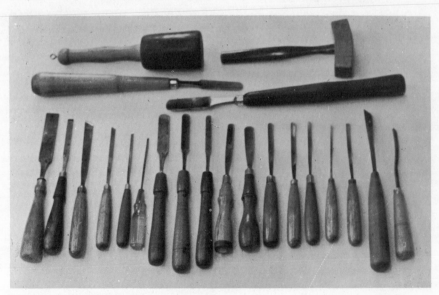

Fig. 4–1 These are the usual carving tools I use in my work. They are listed on the accompanying page.

I show in Fig. 4–1 a few of the tools I have in my collection and the ones shown are those that I use almost all the time for all the many kinds of work I do. They are listed as follows—

From top to bottom and left to right, these carving tools are:

Rosewood driving mallet			
Tiger maple tapping mallet			
Butcher's	11/16″	#2	Straight gouge
Butcher's	1″	#3	Straight gouge

These tools above are positioned under the mallets.

Hargrave	1″		Paring chisel, straight
Hargrave	3/8″		Straight chisel
Buck Bros.	5/8″		Skew chisel
Buck Bros.	3/8″		Skew chisel
Buck Bros.	3/16″		Skew chisel
Addis	1/8″		Spear chisel
Greaves	3/4″	#2	Straight gouge
Greaves	5/8″	#2	Straight gouge
Greaves	7/16″	#2	Straight gouge
Addis	7/16″	#5	Straight gouge
Addis	11/16″	#3	Straight gouge
Addis	3/8″	#12	Longbent gouge
Addis	5/16″	#15	Longbent gouge
Addis	1/4″	#12	Longbent gouge
Addis	1/4″	#12	Longbent chisel
Addis	1/8″	#12	Longbent chisel
Addis	1/2″	#41	Parting tool, straight
Addis	3/16″	#42	Parting tool, longbent

One more set of tools is almost a must as you get involved in this business, and that is a set of rifflers. These are specially shaped and toothed files. Add to them a wood rasp and a fine cut wood file and you are all set. A few bench clamps are useful, too. All these tools are shown in Figs. 4–2.

Fig. 4–2 Carver's rifflers on handy homemade stand with rasp and file shown in front. I forgot the clamps!

5
Bench Tools

I use the term bench tools to differentiate between the usual hand tools most men and some women have to use for the odd jobs around the house and the more or less expert (sic) carpentry jobs that come up, and the carving tools most woodcarvers have to learn to use.

A photograph of a few of the bench tools I use frequently and that complement the carving tools previously shown may be a reminder that if you have none of these, or only some of them, it might be wise to get them because in the course of this short work on carving I may describe and picture these tools being used for various purposes. Fig. 5–1

I might give you a tip—when you clamp a piece of carving to the bench top, in the rough or completely bosted out, be sure you place a small piece of material between the end of the clamp and the surface of the work in question. Otherwise, the clamp-end will mar the surface. I keep a supply of odd sized pieces of $1/8''$ hardboard on hand for this purpose and use these bits, as will be seen in some of the following pictures.

There are a great many more bench tools that you will want to buy and master before you are done with woodcarving but neither space nor time permit their listing at the moment.

Fig. 5–1 Bench tools usually used in the workshop.

6
Sharpening Edged Tools

Special techniques are required to sharpen edged tools such as a firmer chisel or plane iron.

Use a double faced stone, preferably one with a coarse face as well as a fine face. Be sure it is an oil stone. If the tool to be sharpened is dull, start with the coarse face first.

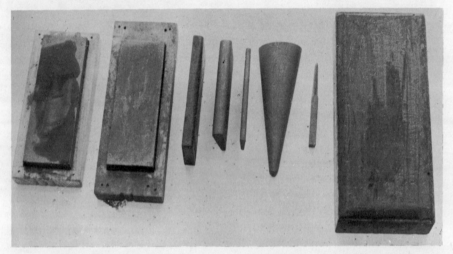

Fig. 6–1 Oilstone, fine and coarse grit faced, hone, gouge slips, leather strop.

Load the stone with light machine oil—#10 motor oil is good for this. (To *Load* means to thoroughly rub oil into the pores of a stone and wipe the surplus off with a rag.) The purpose of the oil is to float the grinding particles off the stone so that it does not get filled and glazed with them.

Place the bevel side of the tool down on the stone, holding the tool at an angle of about thirty degrees from the horizontal. The edge of the tool should be close to the end of the stone nearest you. Then with some care and light but firm pressure move the edge along the stone toward the far end of the stone. The edge should be at a slight skew (angle) to the long dimension of the stone.

Lift the tool clear of the stone and resume the first position. Then again move the tool away from you as before. Repeat this process three or four times more until you turn up the *burr*. The *burr* is a roughness along the edge of the tool. It is a series of very small hook-like bits of tool steel and can be felt with the finger as you test the edge for this very thing. Once the burr is turned up, turn the tool over, face side down on the stone. Hold

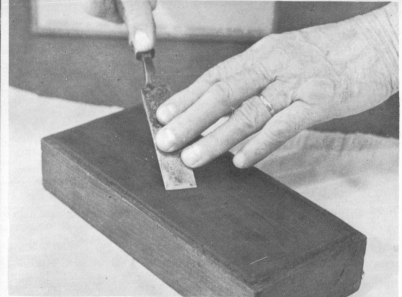

Left, Fig. 6–2 Oilstoning firmer chisel. Bevel side on stone—note skew of chisel on stone. Tool is moved away from person. Right: Fig. 6–3 Oilstoning face—or flat side of chisel—note skew tool is being moved away from person.

the tool flat on the stone with some slight pressure and move the tool forward along the stone, being sure you start, as before, at the edge of the stone nearest you. Again, hold the edge at a slight skew.

Once or twice more, pass the tool along the stone. After so doing, the burr probably will be turned to the bevel side.

Next, turn the stone over, fine side up, load that side with oil. Proceed as described above; it will probably take three or four passes before the burr (this time much less noticeable) is turned up on the face side of the tool. Once the burr is turned, turn the tool over face down and make the necessary passes along the stone. The burr should be reduced. If not, alternate the bevel and the face side, one pass on the stone each until the burr is ground off.

Next, oil up a proper slip—a *hone* in this case—your tool being a straight edged tool. The *hone* is a fine India or Arkansas stone of about four or five inches long and perhaps three inches wide. Use the hone in exactly the same manner as you did the oil stone, except make only two or, at the outside, three passes on the hone, alternating the tool's edge as it is being honed.

Above, Fig. 6–4 Honing bevel of firmer chisel—note slight skew. Right, Fig. 6–5 Honing face of firmer chisel.

Next, strop the edge up on the strop, which is usually a piece of sole leather fastened to a wooden block with brads at the corners, the heads of the brads being set below the surface of the leather. The strop ought to be about ten inches long and perhaps four inches wide. It should be well loaded with a mixture of light oil and emery flour, this about #300 grit. Be sure it is well rubbed into the surface of the strop.

In stropping up a tool, the reverse of the stoning procedure is followed for obvious reasons: You can't push a tool along the leather. However, the tool is held at the same angle and skew as you draw it to you along the leather. Again, alternate the faces of the tool on the strop.

Left, Fig. 6–6 Stropping bevel side of firmer chisel. Tool being drawn towards person of course! Right, Fig. 6–7 Stropping face side of firmer chisel—again drawn towards person.

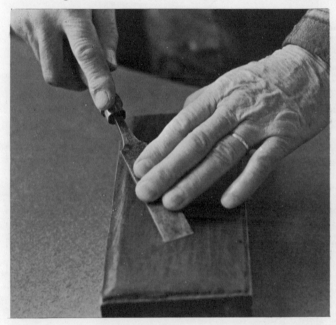

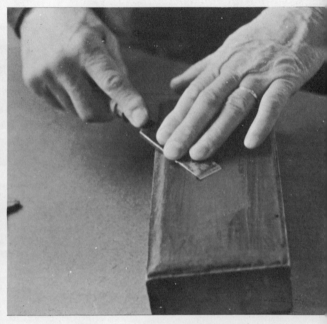

If you are sharpening any of the gouges or the other carving shapes, the procedures outlined above will pertain in so far as the bevel edge of the tool is concerned. However, it is necessary to see that the tool is slowly rotated about its axis as it passes along the sharpening stone so that all parts of the edge come in contact with the surface of the oil stone. But there is a slight difference. It is this—the tool is pushed on the stone, starting with one, the right-hand corner of the tool resting on the surface. It is rotated to the left as it is moved forward.

Below, Fig. 6–8 Sharpening plane iron, fine stone. Note: The plane iron is held at skew to face of stone. Right, Fig. 6–9 Sharpening bevel side of gouge on oilstone.

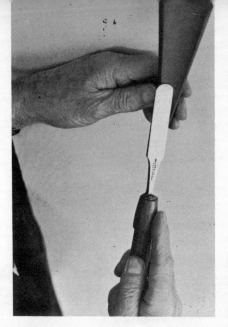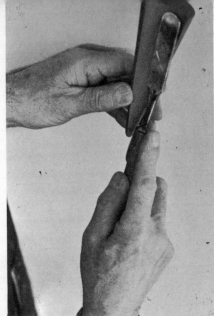

Right, Fig. 6–10 First position of gouge on tapered slip— honing up edge. Left, Fig. 6–11 Second position of gouge. Tool is rotated right to left in this process.

On the second pass, the tool is held with the left-hand corner on the stone and as it is moved forward, it is rotated to the right. Again, the purpose is to turn up a burr and after this is done, use the India stone gouge slip (the large tapered slip shown in the photograph) to remove the burr or turn the burr as the case may be. When the gouge is honed, these same processes are carried out; likewise when it is stropped, except in this instance, the tool is pulled toward you on the leather.

The final steps in sharpening all edged tools lie in the care with which the work of sharpening is done and, most importantly, the care you take to see the tool is not nicked in use or otherwise abused.

If you will keep the following lines more or less in mind, you cannot go wrong in sharpening edged tools:

Oil stone, bevel down, oil stone, bevel up. Slip, bevel down, slip, bevel up. Hone, bevel down, hone, bevel up. Strop, bevel down and pull, strop, bevel up and also pull.

The photographs accompanying this chapter are numbered in sequence according to the directions in the paragraph just above and clearly show the techniques involved.

Fig. 6–12 Bevel side of gouge has been stropped; face side of gouge being stropped on the edge of the strop. The blade is pulled, not pushed.

7
The Kinds
of Carvings

Woodcarvings are made in the following forms or combinations of these forms, as the woodcarver may choose.

Carvings in the round are those in which all three dimensions are developed in the final form. This is frequently termed "wood sculpture." A dolphin carved in this manner is shown in Fig. 7–1.

Fig. 7–1 A dolphin carved in the round.

A freehand drawing that illustrates the terms commonly used to describe the other forms of carvings is shown, and in this drawing the one lettered "A" shows the form termed *alto rilievo,* meaning high relief. Fig. 7–2A

Mezzo relievo is shown in Fig. 7–2B. This form is in moderate relief.

Bas relievo carvings are done as shown in Fig. 7–2C. These carvings are called "low reliefs."

Cameo carvings are commonly not used in any considerable degree unless they are to be part of another form and are done as a matter of contrast. This form is shown in Fig. 7–2D. It is almost without elevation. The best example I can think of is that of a newly minted coin.

The term *intaglio* refers to a carving all of which is done below the surrounding surface, a sunken form, if you will. This is shown in Fig. 7–2E and below is a cross-section.

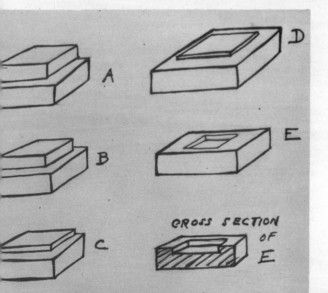

Fig. 7–2 Several kinds of relief carvings.

19

The various photographs that accompany this part are clearly identified as to form and kind of carving in their captions.

These forms may be combined in a carving such as is shown in the detail of carving Fig. 7–6 where the main subject is carved mezzo relievo and the minor comment—that is—the helmets and bayonets are carved cameo.

Top left, Fig. 7–3 Study in mahogany for "Mermaid of Copenhagen" carved in the round. Left, Fig. 7--4 Brig panel carved alto relievo. Bottom left, Fig. 7–5 Side picture of brig panel detail showing depth of alto relievo. Above, Fig. 7–6 Portion of the panel "Victory for a Tattered Banner" carved mezzo relievo; helmets and broken bayonets carved cameo. Below, Fig. 7–7 Pair of nesting Canadian geese. Polychromed panel carved mezzo relievo.

8
Designs and Techniques for Woodcarvings

Keep the design for your first woodcarving as simple as you can because there is nothing more discouraging than to attempt a piece of work on which the details are far beyond your present skills.

I suggest the first project you undertake is the scallop shell (shown in Fig. 9–1). Many of the techniques you wish to learn are included in this simple piece.

To help you understand the terminology used in carving, what follows may be of help.

Bosting out. Used to describe the work of removing all the stock about a design that is not to be incorporated in the final piece.

Stop cuts. Cuts made vertically into a piece for the purpose of outlining the design and also to prevent other tools to be used from overrunning the edges of the design.

Back cuts. These are cuts made with a gouge or other carving tool diagonally into the stock towards the stop cuts already made always on the waste-stock side of the design. The first series of back cuts, as well as stop cuts, should be made lightly and easily. They need not be forced with great effort.

Back cuts are used as a means of showing where the processes involved in bosting out are to be undertaken.

Running cuts. These are more or less continuous cuts made to develop the detail of a carving once the stop and back cuts have been done and the piece is ready for detail carving. Depending upon the kind of detail being developed, these cuts may be made with a skew chisel. A *veiner* may be used for these cuts. A *veiner* is v-shaped with cutting edges on each side of the "v" at the end of the tool. In some catalogues, it is listed as a fluting tool. The cut may be made with a parting tool or it may be made with any other narrow bladed, smallish tool in the carver's box.

Stopping off or *bottoming off cuts*, both mean the same, are usually made after all the rest of the cuts necessary to develop the form of the relievo carvings are done. The purpose of these cuts is to dress up, so to speak, the background surrounding the relief work and eliminate the odd tool scores or marks on the background where tools have overrun the design's edges.

These are the basic terms applied to the art of carving and the manner in which these cuts are made and their purposes are shown and illustrated in the succeeding parts of this small work.

There is no secret in how a carving is designed. The matter is not complicated nor need it be. My procedure is quite simple.

First, decide the kind of carving you want to make and the purpose it is to serve, if any. Then, choose the most suitable wood. Next, make the drawing more or less to fit the purpose. All the details that are going to be incorporated in the final piece should be shown on the original drawing as best you can.

If the piece being designed is larger than the stock on hand, especially if it is wider, stock can be "jointed up," that is, two pieces of stock glued up edge to edge to develop the proper width.

If the carving is to be a compound carving, that is, one in which more than one piece of stock is involved, be sure the extra stock is readily at hand or available.

I suggest you keep one matter in mind when designing a carving of a natural object, a bird, flower, shell, or what have you—nature never repeats herself. She abhors straight lines and symmetry.

In the following, I will show and describe in detail several carvings. Among them is a scallop shell on a panel which later will be gilded. There will be three eagles, a dolphin in the round, and several other decorative pieces. Nearly all the techniques you will need to develop are involved in these carvings. Photographs and their captions will explain them more fully than the text.

You will find that it is necessary for you to learn how to "read the grain of the wood" and so, anticipate the need to change either the method, tool or the tool's attitude in its relationship to the piece of stock upon which you are working.

Always when possible, use the tools with the run of the grain, that is, in the direction toward which the grain runs.

If your design calls for several cuts across the grain of the wood, make the cuts lightly and be sure the edge of the tool is at least razor-sharp.

9
Carving a Sea-scallop Shell

When you want to make a woodcarving, first decide what the subject matter will be, how big the piece is to be and the kind of wood from which it will be made. Then decide what tools are to be used. I suggest the sea-scallop shell as a simple starter.

Draw the design on paper, making sure the subject is within your capacity to make. Show some of the details in this drawing. Fig. 9–1

Fig. 9–1 Full size drawing of sea scallop shell, 9" x 12"

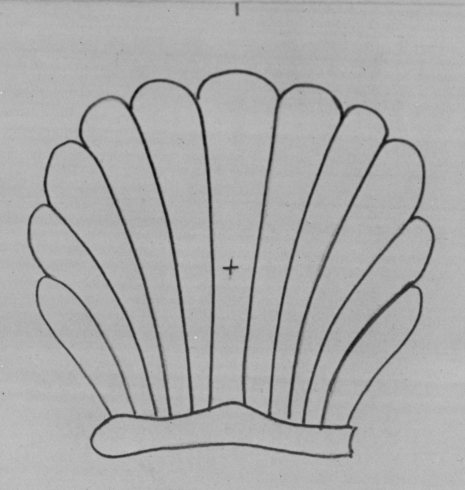

23

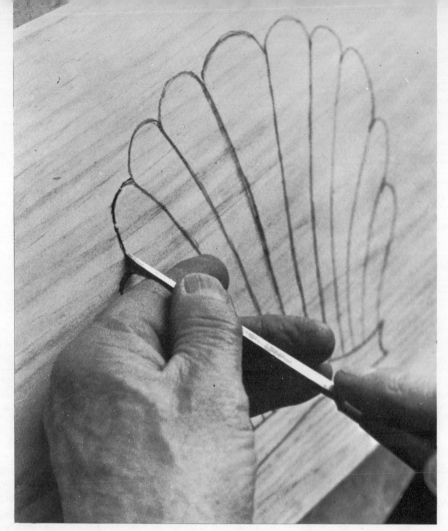

Fig. 9–2 Drawing has been traced onto block. With a 1/4" skew chisel, stop cutting has been started in order to outline the scallop shell.

Select a piece of stock from your stockpile and clip it to the approximate dimensions shown on your drawing. Plane one face smooth and square up the ends.

Thumbtack the drawing on the stock, place carbon paper under it and trace the drawing off onto the wood, Fig. 9–2. The stock used in the illustrations for this piece is native white pine, reasonably clear and straight grained. It is ³/₄" thick, 9" wide and 12" long.

Remove the drawing, darken the carbon outlines with a soft pencil, mount the stock on a plywood back-up, and clamp the whole thing to the bench top.

Except for specific mention of dimensions and materials, the routine just outlined above is that which you will probably follow in all cases where you are to make a carving in any of the relievo forms from a piece of wood of the proper kind and size.

Note—when you use white pine for a carving, it is seldom necessary to mallet a tool into the wood, the characteristic of pine being the relative softness of the material making this unnecessary.

The following terminology will be used throughout the text.

Stop cuts are vertical cuts made with a suitable tool all about the outlilne of a design or a part thereof where other cuts are going to be made. They help emphasize the difference in plane of the part or detail in question.

Back cuts are cuts usually made with a #3 or #5 gouge of reasonable width into the face of the stock, outside the stop cut line and at an angle in toward the stop cut. This being done, as has been mentioned, on the waste-stock side. After making these first cuts to develop the outline, successive cuts of these kinds are made; the stop cuts being made deeper, the back cuts made wider and wider and deeper until the desired dimension has been developed in depth. Figs. 9–3, 9–4, and 9–5

In this problem, use a 3/8" width skew chisel to make the stop cuts all about the outline on the blank.

Top left, Fig. 9–3 First series of stop cuts on outline is completed; back cuts are started. Top right, Fig. 9–4 Making the second series of back cuts on the shell outline. Left, Fig. 9–5 Second series of stop cuts is completed.

Use a ³/₈" #3 or #4 gouge, straight, to make the back cuts, as shown in the preceding photographs. Continue these cuts until the outline cuts are about ³/₈" deep. The back cuts should have, by now, been made about an inch or more away from the stop cuts.

The next step is to "stop-off" the waste material, called in this art, "the waste-stock side." This waste-stock is not incorporated in the finished piece.

The term *stop-off* means that a wider gouge, perhaps a ³/₄" #4 gouge, is used to eliminate this waste-stock, that is, cut it away all about the carving out to the edge of the blank, as in Figs. 9–6 and 9–7.

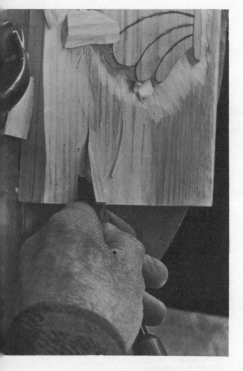

Left, Fig. 9–6 Stopping off waste stock on panel with a 3/4" #3 gouge. Right, Fig. 9–7 Stopping off background away from shell to work with run of grain.

Using a ³/₈" skew chisel held vertically to the face of the panel, make outline cuts all along the lines showing where the ridges are to be developed. Start the tool at the hinge side, that is, the part of the shell that is at the bottom of the panel which, in an actual sea-scallop, is the point at which both parts of the bivalve are joined. Follow all the lines from the hinge to the outside profile.

Using the same tool, make light cuts diagonally along the outline cuts working always with the run of the grain, Fig. 9–8. In this case, these cuts are called clearing cuts, Figs. 9–9, 9–10, and 9–11. Note that in the picture Fig. 9–11, the edges of these diagonal cuts are numbered and the arrows point to the sides of the modelling cuts that are made from the hinge to

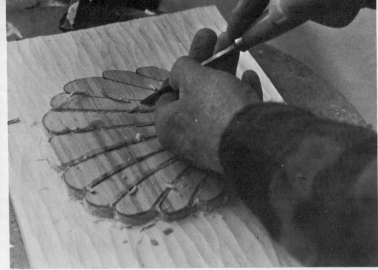

Above left, Fig. 9–8 Stop cuts made along ridge lines are completed; back cuts are started to model the ridge lines. Above right, Fig. 9–9 More back cuts and modelling cuts being made along ridge lines. Note these cuts are made so skew chisel follows run of grain. Below left, Fig. 9–10 Position of carving reversed on bench so skew chisel can be used more handily to make modelling cuts following the grain. Below right, Fig. 9–11 Modelling cuts have been smoothed up on both sides of ridges. Note the numbers; tools will follow these numbers in all further processes.

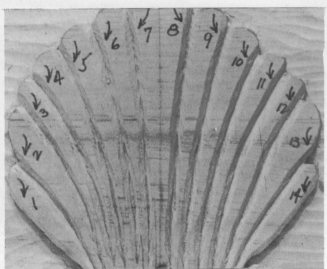

the outer edge of the shell. In Fig. 9–10, the position of the piece has been reversed on the bench so the clearing cuts are more readily made from the shell's outside profile back towards the hinge.

Continue making these two cuts until the desired depth of the detail in the center of the shell has been developed. Bear in mind the shell when completed will have a considerable difference in the depth of the clearing cuts at their ends as compared to the depth at the center of the carving.

Top, Fig. 9–12 Ridges have been partially rounded off with a 1/2″ skew chisel in the sequence as indicated by the numbered ridges. Bottom, Fig. 9–13 Carving of ridges and hinge is completed. A longbent #5 gouge being used for bottoming off the background to complete the carving.

The next step is to round off the details. This is done by carefully cutting away the material at either end of the clearing cuts, and, by so doing, developing the rounding of the surfaces to conform to the structure of a real scallop shell. By using a broader skew than the one used for the clearing cuts just described above, these roundings and modellings can be readily done. Use the tool as if it was a fine set plane, that is, take off very thin chips and try to make the cuts, again, with the run of the grain. Fig. 9–12

The last step in the development of this piece, after the rounding-off of the flutes or ribs of the shell have been completed, is to stop-off or bottom-off the background with the curved longbent gouge #5. This process is shown in Fig. 9–13. In completing this part of the work, it will be necessary for you to be sure you read the grain of the wood and follow the direction in which it runs; otherwise, a general foul-up will be the result of your efforts.

As has already been mentioned, the purpose of stopping-off or bottoming-off is to give the background a finished appearance as well as to eliminate the small blemishes made when your tools have overrun the edges of the shell.

The final appearance of the carving sometimes can be enhanced if a judicious use of fine sandpaper is used to smooth off the more glaring errors of tool use. On the other hand, I suggest you let these stand as is; otherwise, the piece will look as if it had been machine carved rather than the result of a labor of love. Fig. 9–14

Fig. 9–14 The carving is completed.

10
Carving a broad Eagle

The first thing to do is to make up your mind what size the carved eagle is to be and then what sort of wood, or stock, the piece is to be carved from.

In the example described and shown in the following photographs and text, the piece will be 24″ wide, wing tip to wing tip. The height, base to top of the head, will be 9½″ and the stock will be 1⅝″ thick. The material will be Honduras mahogany.

To make the design for this or any other carving where a similarity will prevail between the two sides, lay out a rectangle the same size as the carving. Bisect the sides and the ends of this drawing and show the point at which these lines intersect in the center of the drawing. These are called index points, Fig. 10–1. Draw in the left-hand wing then the left side of the tail and the position of the leg and claw. Trace these lines off, also the index points on the left side of the drawing. Invert the tracing on the opposite side of the drawing, set the index points over the corresponding ones on the right-hand side and center and place carbon paper under the drawing. Trace off the inverted outlines of the wing and tail sections and remove both drawing and carbon. Then darken the lighter lines left by the carbon paper. Next, draw in the head detail as you would like it to be in the finished carving. I suggest you bear this in mind: When the eagle's head is turned over its right-hand shoulder, the head position is said to be in the "dexter" position; when it is turned over the left shoulder, it is in the "sinister" position. This is the heraldic meaning of the bird's head attitude, if that is at all important to you. Fig. 10–1

Fig. 10–1 Outline of drawing of a broad eagle to be carved as Problem #2. Note the index points.

Once you are satisfied with the final design, the following procedure should be carried out. Cut off the piece of stock on which you propose to carve the bird. Be sure the dimensions agree or even are slightly larger than those of the drawing.

If necessary, plane off both faces of the stock.

Index the block if you want to, but be sure in any case the entire drawing can be traced off with carbon paper on the block and, once positioned, so that it is, trace the outlines and what details are shown on your drawing off onto the stock. Remove the drawing and darken the outlines and details so it can be readily seen as you next bandsaw the piece out. Fig. 10–2

Fig. 10–2 Bandsawing on outline of the broad eagle completed.

As you do this operation, be sure you stay outside the outlines of the drawing on the block because you will want some waste stock to trim off and smooth up the actual carving blank all about its exterior with various tools.

Place the blank in the bench vise and pare off the waste stock with skew chisels, rifflers and the spokeshave. Fig. 10–3 Be sure you do not go below the outlines of the piece in this process. The tips of the wing feathers are

Fig. 10–3 Paring off waste stock on feather ends using a 3/8″ skew chisel.

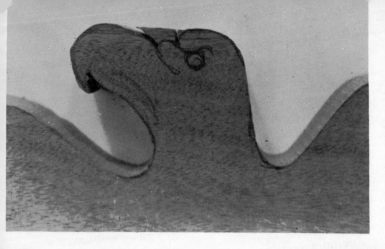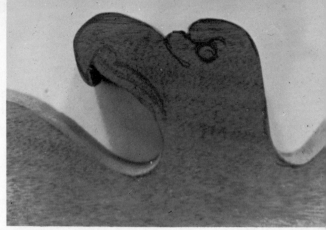

Left, Fig. 10–4 Appearance of head after bandsawing is completed. Right, Fig. 10–5 Paring off of waste stock on head has been completed.

shaped up according to the design lines in this process. Also, the shape of the bird's head is developed in profile.

Mount the finished profiled blank on a plywood back-up, Fig. 10–6, and clamp the assembly to the bench top. Fig. 10–7

Use a #4 or a #5 straight gouge and mallet it in vertically for the stop cuts all about the legs. Then make the back cuts, Fig. 10–7. Continue these cuts, alternating them as required until the legs have been outlined to a depth of about three quarters of an inch.

Start bosting out the wings. In the example illustrated in this book, the first one worked on is the bird's left-hand wing (it makes no difference which one is first, to be sure). Work this bosting out until the depth of the wing curve has been reached; in this case, the thickness of the wing feather

Left, Fig. 10–6 Paring off of the entire profile of the eagle is completed. The eagle is mounted on plywood backup for further carving. Right, Fig. 10–7 Eagle and backup are clamped to bench top, and work of bosting out is begun.

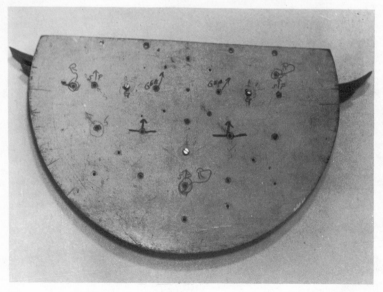

in the center of the lower edge of the wing is about half an inch. Note that all the other feathers slope downward toward this feather from either side, thus giving the curvature needed for the finished piece. Fig. 10–8

Using a pencil compass, take off the thickness of each wing feather end from the back-up to the top of the feather and so, transfer this thickness by marking the end of the corresponding feather on the opposite; i.e., right wing. Fig. 10–9

Left, Fig. 10–8 Eagle's left wing being bosted out. In heraldry, this is the sinister side. In this process, do not cut into the grain. Right, Fig. 10–9 Feather ends of the right wing are scribed in order to indicate the depths of bosting out necessary so that the right wing feathers are the same thickness as their corresponding left wing feathers.

Fig. 10–10 Bosting out is completed on the head, wings, and tail section of the bird.

Bost out the right-hand wing to correspond in cross-section to that of the left wing. Cut down, that is the usual term, the top edge of both wings in the manner shown in Fig. 10–11 and Fig. 10–12. To make them alike, cut down one wing, index the depths of the cuts in a similar position on the opposite wing with the dividers and cut down the edge to this index line, as you did when you marked the bottom edge of the feathers.

The carving should now resemble, vaguely, that shown in Fig. 10–10.

Top, Fig. 10–11 Top edges of the wing are cut down slightly to develop the two curves shown in Fig. 10–9, and the depth of the back cutting on the reverse side is indicated by the dark line. Bottom, Fig. 10–12 Back cutting the reverse side of the eagle.

Next, scribe the line shown on the edges of the feathers, Fig. 10–11, by removing the carving from the back-up and using your fingers as a gauge (a trick you will have to learn) make the line all about the entire profile of the carving. This line should be about ³⁄₈″ below the bosted surface of the piece. This is the line to which you will reduce the stock on the back of the carving with various tools, gouges, spokeshaves and chisels, as best fit the needs. The purpose is to make the carving more or less lifelike in this particular instance. This is shown in Fig. 10–12.

Top, Fig. 10–13 Back cutting completed. Bottom, Fig. 10–14 Both the design lines for the feathering out and for the detail carvings of the bird are drawn in.

Next, model the back of the bird's head so it will be similar to the finished side, but without all the detail that the finished product will have. After the back of the head is modelled up, turn the carving over and clamp it to the bench top. Then, with great care, finish the detail carving of the head, the beak, the cere, the eye and nostril and eyefold. Before this work is done, be sure you have outlined all these details. The processes are shown in Figs. 10–15 and 10–16.

Left, Fig. 10–15 Carving the beak is part of the detail carving done to develop the head of the eagle. Right, Fig. 10–16 Carving of eagle's head is completed.

Remount the carving on the plywood back-up and then model the legs, in the manner shown in Fig. 10–15, with a three-quarter inch #3 gouge. Complete both legs in a similar manner and make them as alike as possible.

Work on the portion of the legs between the ends of the feathering and the claws with a 1/4″ skew chisel and a 1/4″ #3 or #4 gouge, and then model out the outline of the claws. These two processes are shown in Figs. 10–17 and 10–18.

Next is to develop the outline of the claws as shown in Fig. 10–18. Be sure that you use great care in this bit of fancywork because the wood sections are brittle and if the tools you use, a spear and a longbent 1/8″ chisel, are twisted, the sections will be fractured. Make all vertical cuts with the spear and pare off the stock inside these cuts with the longbent chisel.

Left, Fig. 10–17 Modelling the legs of the eagle. Right, Fig. 10–18 The waste stock has been removed from between the ends of the eagle's leg feathers and the tops of its claws. One claw outline is shown being carved.

Above, Fig. 10–19 Further development of claw outlines. Top right, Fig. 10–20 More development of the claws. Center right, Fig. 10–21 Feathering of legs is completed. Details of the claws are being done with considerable care! Bottom right, Fig. 10–22 Both claws are completed

The next step is to draw in all the feathers you wish to show on the finished piece. Make the outlines of these on each wing freehand as well as the feathers on each leg and the body. You will in all probability find that these lines can be drawn more readily if the bird is removed from the back-up. This bit is shown in Fig. 10–14.

Remount the carving on the back-up and detail the feathering on each leg before you do further work.

After the preceding work is done, model up the claw details in the manner shown in Fig. 10–20 using a ¼″ or a 5/16″ longbent gouge—either a #3 or a #15 shape will do the job. Use great care in this detail work, as in all the rest of the detail that is involved on this piece, because all you need to do is to twist the tool once and that is that.

When done, the ends of the claws may look not unlike those shown in Fig. 10–22.

To develop the feathers, use first the ½″ parting tool wherever possible and on the smaller sections, use the ¼″ parting tool. It is necessary to be sure you follow the run of the grain of the wood. The first step in feathering out is shown in Fig. 10–23. The smaller parting tool can be used advantageously on the feathers on either side of the body and the adjacent wing sections, Fig. 10–24, as well as on the tail feathers. Use the 1/4" parting tool to model the body feathers. Fig. 10–25

Once all the feathers are outlined, model them up with suitable gouges of various sizes. Be sure that when this is done the effect will be that the feathers overlap. This is done by modelling the lower portion of each feather slightly below that of the top of the feather next below. Fig. 10–26

As you work on the feathering, you will see where certain cuts need to be smoothed up on the carving. Some errors in tool manipulation will be seen, these are unavoidable, and these errors of skill and judgment can be corrected by the judicious use of gouges and rifflers.

Top left, Fig. 10–23 Using the 1/2" parting tool to outline wing feathers. Top right, Fig. 10–24 Using parting tool to outline feathers on wing portion adjacent to eagle's body. Bottom left, Fig. 10–25 Using the parting tool to outline the body feathers. Bottom right, Fig. 10–26 How the eagle's feathers are modelled so as to appear as if they are overlapping.

Fig. 10–27 Carving is finished.

As a final touch and to finish up the carving, I suggest you make up a mixture of raw linseed oil, some small quantity, perhaps a fifth of that volume of turpentine and a dight of Japan dryer. Apply this to the finished carving; then hang the piece up on the wall of the shop to dry out for a couple of weeks. When that has taken place, apply a good stout floor wax to the carving, rub it in briskly and then take it into the house, give it to your wife and she will either point to it with pride or throw it out the door. Fig. 10–27

11
Carving a Dolphin in the Round

The term, "carving in the round," means that the piece is to be carved in all three of its dimensions. Fig. 11–1

Fig. 11–1 A dolphin carved in the round.

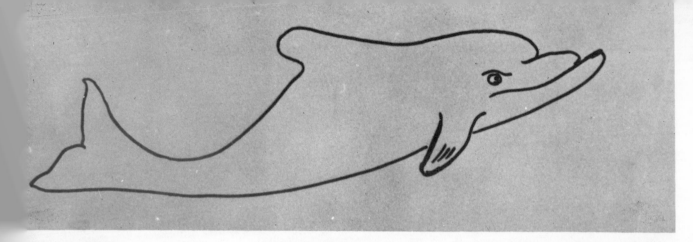

Fig. 11–2 Outline drawing for dolphin.

A dolphin may be one of the more simple forms of this sort of carving; therefore, I suggest you design one and your problem will then be to execute the piece.

The techniques that will be applied to this piece are those that will be used to a great extent on any other form of this sort. If you must be a "purist," you may call the work sculpture in wood; but in my mind, this dresses the woodcarving art up in fancy duds.

No massive gouges nor mallets will be used on the piece you are about to undertake; these are not required.

I think you will be wise if your first piece is made from a good clear, straight grained piece of white pine; forget the more fancy and expensive woods until you have mastered some of the necessary skills. The stock ought to be about 25" long, 5 to 6" wide and 2" thick.

In life, the dolphin's tail is about one and one half times wider than is his body; therefore, some compromise in design and structure will be required. See and ponder on Figs. 11–9, 11–11, and 11–15.

Smooth the stock up with the hand plane, lay down your design on the block with tracing paper with carbon paper under that. Be sure the design will be within your skills to make, of course.

Fig. 11–3 Bandsawing out dolphin. Note waste stock.

Set the bandsaw to clear the stock. Using a fine-toothed blade, bandsaw out the two pieces, the base and the dolphin's body. Be sure you stay on the waste-side of your design. Fig. 11–3

By using the spokeshave, the various skew chisels and gouges as may fit the various curves, smooth up the profiles of each piece to the design lines. When the smooth profiles are developed, it will be necessary to provide the means whereby the two parts are to be joined. This will be done by using a ½" by 2" long hardwood dowel. I think you will be ahead of the game in the future if you buy the necessary tools with which to make the dowels and to bore the holes for their reception.

A ½" diameter shanked, ½" diameter lipped brad point boring tool can usually be bought from a good hardware store; also a dowel and plug cutter of the same diameter can be or should be bought as well. If your local store does not carry these items, he can, if he will and wishes to, get them for you. If you do not have a drill press in your shop, you can get these tools to fit portable drills with half inch capacity chucks.

Here let me say that the outer surfaces of the wave form can be smoothed up on the outside with the spokeshave. The inner curve can be smoothed up with the various rifflers used judiciously. Then sand off the tool marks made by these files. Be sure you break all the sharp edges on this piece before you go further. Do this with #120 sandpaper.

Locate the holes for the dowel in this manner—first, hold the dolphin on the base, i.e., the wave form, in the position you desire it to be when the carving is completed. Mark the sides of both pieces lightly at the exact point of contact. Use the trysquare and square these two indexed points across the faces of each piece. The index point is, of course, that point at which you made the mark on the sides of each piece. Fig. 11–4

Fig. 11–4 Squaring up guideline prior to boring hole for dowel.

Locate the exact longitudinal center of each of the two parts on the line just squared up and prickpoint that center exactly. Use care in so doing for it is at that point where the two holes for the dowel will be bored. Use the trysquare and mark a vertical line from the base or bottom of the wave block at the index point where the two parts will be in contact. Place the block on the drill press and see that the point of the boring tool is exactly on the center-punched hole before you bore the hole for the dowel. Fig. 11–5

Left, Fig. 11–5 Squaring across body of carving for index point at which boring tool point will be placed. Right, Fig. 11–6 Dolphin clamped on squared block prior to boring dowel hole. Boring tool is run down vertical line to check proper positioning of body.

The dowel hole need not be deeper than an inch. Bore this accordingly.

So that the dolphin will be located exactly as it has been indexed, use a squared-up clamp block small enough so it will be out of the way of the drill point, yet long enough to give proper support to the dolphin's body as it is being drilled. Then, clamp the body block on this squared-up block and place both parts on a plane surface (a flat surface). Using either a drafting triangle or the trysquare placed beside the body of the dolphin so the edge of the tool rests exactly on the side indexed point, draw a vertical line along the edge of the tool. Fig. 11–6

It may be necessary to make a small adjustment to the position of the dolphin's body to be sure the vertical line is, again, exactly lined up with the cross-body line, as in Fig. 11–6.

Next, place these two assembled pieces on the drill press beside the boring tool; then run this tool down along the vertical line on the side of the dolphin, making sure the point follows the line in its entirety. If it does not, ease up on the clamp, adjust the position of the body block and then recheck the travel of the tool's point. Once the body block is

Left, Fig. 11–7 Boring dowel hole in dolphin. Right, Fig. 11–8 Boring of dowel hole in wave support is started.

properly located, bring the brad point of the boring tool down on the center punch mark and bore the hole; do not bore too deeply or the tool will pass through the dolphin's body. I think a hole about $3/4''$ deep will be sufficient. Fig. 11–7

Shape up the body of the dolphin first by using the spokeshave, Fig. 11–9, as well as the rifflers where necessary. I suggest you pare the body off to an approximate round with a broad gouge before you use the spokeshave to smooth it up back of the dorsal fin; it's easy to do this if you use some care and follow the run of the grain. Once the gouge has removed all the waste-stock, except enough left to finish up smoothly with the shave, saw out the dorsal fin slightly wider than it is to be in the final piece; do this with a backsaw. I show how I saw out the flippers in Fig. 11–18. This same technique is used on the dorsal fin.

Use a round riffler to shape up the base of the dorsal fin, as in Fig. 11–10. Use a $1/2''$ skew chisel to shape up the sides of the dorsal fin to its final dimension. This, by the way, should look like an elongated oval in cross-section, narrow end toward the head of the beast.

Left, Fig. 11–9 Shaping up and rounding off body of dolphin with spoke-shave. Right, Fig. 11–10 Dorsal fin has been cut down on both sides. Round riffler being used to shape this part up.

Top left, Fig. 11–11 Rough cuts on tail section are made with gouge. Top right, Fig. 11–12 Bosting out one side of tail section. Bottom left, Fig. 11–13 Bosting out second side of tail section. Body of dolphin has been reversed for this second process. Bottom right, Fig. 11–14 Working with riffler on opposite side of dorsal fin.

The next step is to rough carve the tail section of the piece with the broad gouge, i.e., the ³/₄″ #3. See Fig. 11–11. Then shape up the final detail of this part with the spokeshave.

The sides of the dorsal fin next to the body are finally finished by shaping up with a fine round riffler. Fig. 11–14. Bear in mind this is not the final work to be done on these sections.

Next, carve out the tail detail. This area to be carved is fragile and you

Fig. 11–15 Bosting out reverse side of tail section. Note wedge under opposite side.

Left, Fig. 11–16 Back and dorsal fin have been rounded off and shaped. Details of head carving have been limned out. Right, Fig. 11–17 Carving mouth of dolphin with 3/8" skew chisel.

cannot make massive cuts with the various gouges you will use. Be sure that you wedge up the tail section, Fig. 11–5, to prevent its fracture.

Draw in the head detail. These details are shown in Fig. 11–16.

Carve these out, round the head down to the desired shape. Fig. 11–17

Turn the block over and follow the procedure shown in Figs. 11–18 and 11–19 to develop the shape of the flippers. This is next to the last work you will do on the piece. If you have lined out the shape of the flippers before you undertake this process, be sure you allow waste-stock on both sides, inside and out, of the flippers so they can be formed up as they are shown to be in Fig. 11–19. Be sure you do not score the belly of the piece with the backsaw. This is too easily done if you are not careful. The final shape of the flippers can be developed with a small ½″ gouge if you use care in its manipulation. The inside surface of the flippers can be roughly shaped up with a flat riffler. I suggest the thickness of each of these parts be not much more than ¼″.

Fig. 11–18 Backsawing down either side of flippers. Do not scratch belly of dolphin with saw.

Fig. 11–19 Completing form of flippers with riffler. All work on these two parts should be done with various shapes of rifflers.

Before you assemble the dolphin and the base together, I suggest you remove with fine sandpaper or a fine riffler or round file the coarser tool marks left from the various cuts made in carving the form out. I prefer to leave some of the tool marks to give texture to the piece. However, do not allow these to dominate the final carving.

To assemble these two parts, ring the inside of the two dowel holes with Duco cement, force the dowel into the base. Then, being sure you have pushed it down to the bottom of the hole, place the dolphin over the top of the dowel and force that down in place, too. Be sure the sides of the two parts are parallel. Be sure the belly of the dolphin touches the top of the base. Set the assembly aside until the next day.

Check the whole business for irregularities you can cure with sandpaper or fine files. Be sure all hard edges are broken with sandpaper. This means this—a hard edge is one in which the edge of the wood is sharp and where the corners are sharp as well, so much so they can scratch your hands if not carefully handled. Breaking the corners and edges means that you develop a very small radius on all these parts. This can best be done with sandpaper folded in quarters.

Finally (a lovely word) apply a light brown stain to the wood, assuming you have used pine for the carving, so that the raw look is done with. Then, when the stain is dry, apply a coat of shellac; let that dry, then use fine steel wool to reduce the shellac to a smooth finish; apply another coat, rub that back with steel wool dipped in linseed oil. Let that dry a day or two and then rub up a soft flowing polish with a soft cotton cloth, give the piece to your "Old Lady" and hope she does not throw it out the door.

12
Making Rope and Other Moldings

Several illustrations that accompany this chapter show how rope molding can be used to decorate pieces of furniture and to embellish mirror frames.

This molding is best made in a series of steps, each one undertaken and completed the full length of the stock before the next step is started.

The processes are as follows: use dividers and determine the center line of the piece of stock; scribe this line its entire length. Set the dividers so the points are equally distant to the width of the stock and then step off the index points. Fig. 12–1

Set your bevel square at an angle of about 40 degrees from the horizontal and scribe an angled line across the stock at each of the indexed points. Fig. 12–2

Place stock in bench vise and using the backsaw, make saw scarfs down each diagonal line to a depth of not over 3/16", holding the sawblade vertical to the edge of the stock. Fig. 12–3

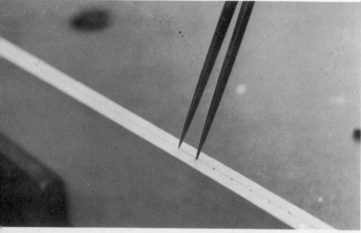

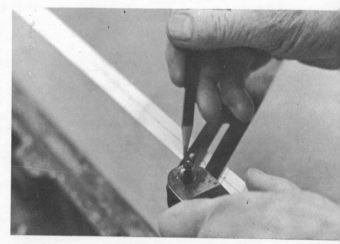

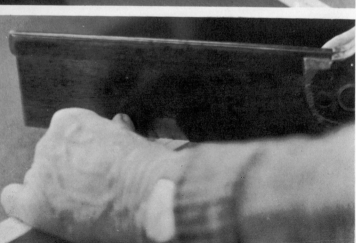

Above left, Fig. 12–1 Indexing points for "lay" of rope molding cuts. Above right, Fig. 12–2 Scribing diagonal lines across index points. Left, Fig. 12–3 Making saw scarfs along diagonals.

Fig. 12–4 Set saw above table top.

Set the rotary sawblade on your sawtable just 3/16″ above the table-top. Move the ripfrence over the width of the stock, Fig. 12–4, by placing the material between the inside edge of the sawblade and the face of the fence. Remove the stock, place it face down on the sawtable with the scribed and diagonally cut edge hard up against the ripfence and start the saw; then make a saw scarf the entire length of the piece.

Then place the stock in the bench vise and make running cuts across the edge following the diagonal lines with the grain and so, start the carving. Once these cuts are made the entire length of the material, reverse the piece, end for end, and make similar cuts along the diagonal lines, opposed to the first series of cuts just made. Figs. 12–5 and 12–6

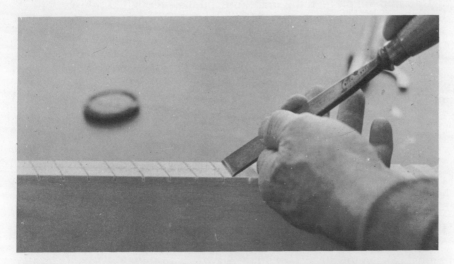

Top, Fig. 12–5 Making first modelling cut on edge of stock. Bottom, Fig. 12–6 Making second series of diagonal cuts with skew chisel.

After both sets of diagonal cuts are completed, use the $1/2''$ skew chisel and carefully cut off the corners of the diagonal cuts on the side on which you made the long saw scarf. Cut these off to the depth of the saw scarf made across the edge of the stock.

Take out of the vise and make a series of pencil lines from the throat of the cuts just made to the saw scarf on the face of the stock. Do this with the skew square set at an angle of about 40 degrees. Fig. 12–7

Backsaw along these lines to a depth of about 3/16'' from the throat to the long saw scarf. Before this, clamp the stock to the face of the workbench. Hold the backsaw at an angle of 30 degrees from the perpendicular to your left. Fig. 12–8

Keep it in mind that each of these cuts is made one after another the entire length of the stock.

Make running cuts from the throat to the saw scarf along each of the diagonal lines just drawn in, and then cut with the backsaw.

Turn the stock end for end on the bench, put wedges under the side with the cuts and clamp the whole thing to the bench, Fig. 12–9; then with the skew chisel, make cuts from the saw scarf to the edge along these diagonals. Fig. 12–10

Unclamp the piece, put it in the vise, partially modelled side away from you, and with the firmer plane, make a chamfer along the far edge lightly, just enough to develop the rough shape of the final edge. Fig. 12–11

Next, start the modelling cuts to develop the final form of the molding.

Be sure the $1/2''$ skew chisel is razor sharp during this process. Start these cuts with the skew held at an angle of about 30 degrees to your right and make the running cut from the edge of the stock nearest you to the farther edge, rotating the tool slightly along the run to your right, Fig. 12–11. These cuts are usually called "rolling cuts."

Carry this cut along the edge and then carefully down the side of the stock to the longitudinal saw scarf. Do not try to take off all the material at once, be satisfied with light cuts as you work on these, otherwise, you will flatten out the sides and lose the appearance of a quarter round piece of rope. I suggest that only one light pass be made on these first cuts. Complete them the entire length of the stock. Fig. 12–12

Then, remove the stock from the vise and place face side up, the diagonal cuts on this surface running away from you. Put wedges under the far edge, Fig. 12–13, clamp the piece to the bench and start rolling cuts similar to those you have just completed at the long saw scarf and move the tool toward the edge, Fig. 12–10. Then, still with the rolling (or rotary) motion of the tool, carry the cut across the edge of the piece and so complete the first of the two or three more passes with the chisel you will have to make before the finished modelling cuts are completed. Make the roll edge with the firmer plane. Fig. 12–11

Once these are done, fold a piece of sandpaper, #110 grit, and using

Above left, Fig. 12–7 Scribing diagonal guidelines on the face of stock from throat of edge cuts to saw scarf. Above right, Fig. 12–8 Using backsaw to make cuts for lay of rope molding on face of stock. Left, Fig. 12–9 Making first of modelling cuts on face of stock along saw scarfs. Below left, Fig. 12–10 Stock is clamped to bench top over wedges. The second series of modelling cuts are shown being made. Below right, Fig. 12–11 Planing off and rounding up edge of molding. Bottom left, Fig. 12–12 Shows position of skew chisel making the second series of modelling cuts. Bottom right, Fig. 12–13 Second series of modelling cuts are completed. Note position of wedge.

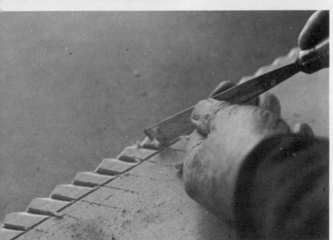

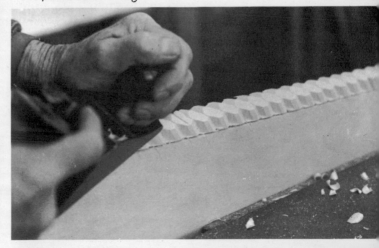

Left, Fig. 12–14 Making saw scarfs for beginning of rope molding on top part of the mahogany epergne. Right, Fig. 12–15 Modelling cuts being made on edge of the epergne to develop final shape of the rope molding.

some care and not too much brute strength, smooth up the carved surfaces to eliminate some, not all, of the tool marks.

Set the sawtable ripfence over the exact distance from the inside of the sawblade that the saw scarf has been made so the two dimensions equal each other. Slowly, and with care, cut the modelled roping from the balance of the material. The sawblade, of course, is set slightly higher than the thickness of the wood.

The last bit to be done is to lightly sand off the sharp edges of the carved rope and to smooth up, again using sandpaper and a sanding block, the just sawed face of the molding. Then, wonder just why on earth you undertook this particular piece, that is, unless you have a specific use for it in your design. For other uses, see Figs. 12–4 through 12–19.

Below, Fig. 12–19 Gardoon border of rope molding for edge of mahogany tiptop table made by author.

Above left, Fig. 12–16 Top of epergne showing completed rope molding. Note: Lightly sand off rough edges and coarse tool marks when finishing this type of molding. Above right, Fig. 12–17 Side elevation of the finished mahogany epergne. Right, Fig. 12–18 Application of rope molding used to trim out stern transom for yacht "Kokua."

In using moldings to decorate simple furniture forms, such as Welsh dressers and so on, it is usual to consider how two or more pieces of molding can complement each other in the final appearance of the piece.

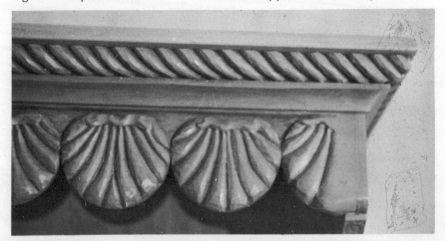

Fig. 12–20 Section of dresser top showing how moldings may be combined to finish off a piece of furniture.

On the dresser top shown in Fig. 12–20, there are three parts above the carved scallop shells. The top section is made with a "breaking," Fig. 12–26, then under this is the rope molding and below that, the cove, another simple form very commonly used in or on furniture. Fig. 12–22

This cove molding is easily made. The steps are as follows:

Plane off and square up the edge of the stock, then plane the face. Set the sawblade on the sawtable about an $1/8''$ above the table top. Set the fence over from the outside; this is emphasized because previously the fence has been set to the inside of the blade. The distance between the fence and the outside of the sawblade should be $3/4''$.

Run the stock through the saw, edge down, then run the stock through the saw, face down. Be sure the piece of wood is about 4" wide because the work you are about to do will be done entirely in the bench vise. Place the stock there, face saw scarf on the inside, i.e., the bench side of the vise.

Left Fig. 12–21 Saw scarfs made prior to carving a piece of cove molding. Right, Fig. 12–22 Use a #7 straight gouge to develop the cove of this molding

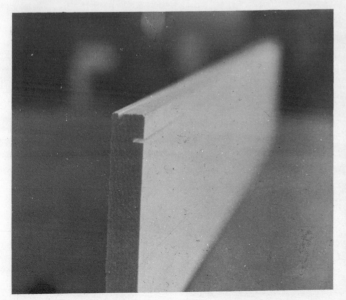

Use a #7 gouge and start the cuts along the edge of the stock, Fig. 12–21. Be sure that the saw scarfs have been made so the grain of the wood runs in the direction in which the work is to be done. Needless to say, if it does not, you are wasting time. These cuts are made one after another the entire length of the piece. As the work shown in Fig. 12–23 is made from a really straight grained piece of wood, long chips can be made with no fear they will run across the piece and so, spoil the outside edge of the finished molding. Continue this process until all of the entire stock has been removed between the two saw scarfs. Fig. 12–24

The finished molding curve will fit the edge of the chisel at the base of the curve, Fig. 12–24. There will be some irregularities, humps and hollows, and these can be eliminated by wrapping a piece of sandpaper around a short length of half inch dowel and then sanding off the inside of the molding. Do not try to get rid of all the tool marks; these add some interest to the texture of the finished piece. Incidentally, these marks show the molding was handmade and so, made with some degree of care and interest. Fig. 12–25

Top, Fig. 12–23 Progress of #7 gouge in making cove molding. Center, Fig. 12–24 Using a #8 gouge to bottom off and finish cove molding. Bottom, Fig. 12–25 Sanding off cove molding with dowel.

The beaking, shown in Fig. 12–26, is made by setting the sawblade ⅛″ above the table top and passing the stock over the saw, the fence being set over about an inch.

Be sure the material has been planed up, side or edge and face.

The second step is to set the fence over so that the outside face of the sawblade coincides with the bottom of the saw scarf just made; the saw is then run up so the top of the teeth coincides with the bottom of the saw scarf. Rip this piece of waste material off, remove the stock from the saw table, put it in the bench vise, edge up and with some care, plane off the edge of the piece to a reasonable radius, one that looks pleasing to your eye. This will vary, of course, according to your choice. Break the opposite edge slightly with sandpaper and then sand off the curved portion of the piece of molding to smooth it up and finish the rounding of the "breaking." Figs. 12–27, 12–28, and 12–29

Above, Fig. 12–26 End of finished beaking molding. Left, Fig. 12–27 Saw scarfs have been made and stock has been ripped off the face of the piece of board for beaking. Below left, Fig. 12–28 Planing off and rounding edge of beaking. Below right, Fig. 12–29 Using a 1/2″ skew chisel to clean up the inner portion of the beaking and so remove saw marks.

All three of these components are used in a variety of ways, sometimes together, sometimes alone. In any event, they are great sources of satisfaction to make and apply.

The techniques to be followed in making the winding cuts discussed on pages 50 and 52 are shown in detail in the photographs in Chapter 18.

13
Application of Carved Moldings

Moldings are generally used to separate the several component plain surfaces of a piece of furniture in a pleasing manner.

In Aromson's *Encyclopedia of Furniture,* the classic Greek and Roman forms of moldings are shown and named as well as some of the post Gothic elaborate forms for architectural use. With some skill and care, a woodcarver can adapt some of these classic forms for his own use; but it has been my experience and observation that the more simple these forms are made, the happier the woodcarver will be with his ideas.

It seems to me that the panels and mirrors I have made and framed with simple forms of moldings, such as I have discussed in the previous chapter, are shown up to greater advantage than they would be dressed up in more formal shapes.

In the several photographs that accompany this chapter, I show various simple moldings applied to pieces of furniture made during the 18th and early 19th centuries, antiques, if you will. These illustrate the point I have made—simplicity in form and shape can be as good if not better than an elaboration of form.

Fig. 13-1 "Hand struck" molding on top of a late 18th century maple highboy made with molding plans.

Above left Fig. 13–2 Corner of the coved handmade stay molding on base of the maple highboy. Above right, Fig. 13–3 Front elevation of the base of a corner cupboard showing use of rope molding both as a border and as a door handle. Made by the author. Below left, Fig. 13–4 Close-up of one corner of the corner cupboard showing a rounded tope edge and the use of hand struck molding to finish off the front edge of the bottom shelf. Note the inverted cove molding trim at the side of the shelf. Below right, Fig. 13–5 Showing use of the molding just described combined with scallop shells carved in the half round to finish off the top of a Welsh dresser.

14
Why Study Pieces for Carvings Are Made

I was once asked to make a replica, 18" tall, of the Gloucester Fisherman that stands on the "hard" at Gloucester, Mass.

I undertook the task, but in order to find out how to best do so, I first made a study piece in pine from the scrap-pile. Fig. 14–1 shows how this study came out, it being designed from a photograph of the wonderful

Left, Fig. 14–1 Study for figure of Gloucester fisherman statue to be carved in the round. Right, Fig. 14–2 Finished carving of the Gloucester fisherman done in mahogany—18" tall.

bronze statue in Gloucester. Fig. 14–2 shows how the finished piece came out after it was made from a block of mahogany of sufficient size, i.e., 5″ thick, 9″ wide and 19″ long.

The study was made to fix the details and to show the obstacles I felt I had to overcome to make the finished piece. The two important points where I thought I could "blow the piece" were the exact attitude of the hands and the arms as the man at the wheel grasped the spokes thereof and also, the semi-crouching attitude of the helmsman as he used all his skill and strength to keep the schooner on course before the full gale that was blowing.

One more reason for the study was that the wheel had to be turned up on the lathe, placed in its exact position on the wheelhousing, and the spokes had to be placed exactly in the proper position so they fitted in the holes in the hands of the helmsman. Tricky stuff.

In Fig. 7–3, I show a study block for a small replica of the "Mermaid of Copenhagen." This study shows some of the pitfalls I had to avoid in the finished piece.

The advantages of the studies are these: Should a mistake be made in your endeavors, you have wasted a bit of talent and that is all, as you throw the poorly executed study out the shop door. If you make a mistake on the final block, you not only have wasted talent and time, but also what can be an expensive block of wood.

Fig. 14–4 Study for a figurehead on a billethead in pine.

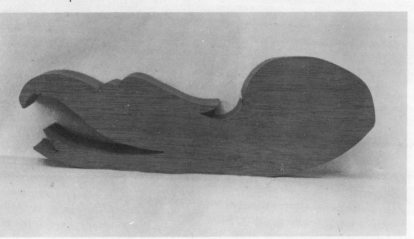

Fig. 14–3 Eagle's head study piece in mahogany.

A study for an eagle's head that had to be made is shown in Fig. 14–3. This was done to develop the proper attitude of the beak. It is a reasonable replica of a carving made of an eagle and shield with two arrows grasped in one claw. The piece was made possibly by Skillins of New York circa 1820, if it can be judged by the techniques shown in the photograph sent me. Fig. 14–4 is a study for a figurehead mounted on a billethead.

Fig. 14–5 Study for figurine
of Paul Bunyon.

Fig. 14–5 is a study for a carving of Paul Bunyan, which I have never finished. Someday I may get time to do so.

In addition to these study pieces, it seems this is an appropriate place to describe the processes involved in making *piercings* for a carving, such as are shown in Figs. 14–6, 14–7, and 14–8. *Piercings* are, of course, holes made purposely in a carving for their decorative effect.

The procedure to make a piercing is this—first bore a hole more or less 1/2″ diameter in the center of the design or that portion that is to be cut away from the balance of the piece. Insert the end of a coping or scroll saw and reconnect it to the sawframe. If you have a mechanical jigsaw, so much the better. Use care in manipulating the saw about the design line, being sure you stay on the waste-stock side of the design. Repeat this process wherever it is necessary until all the piercings are made.

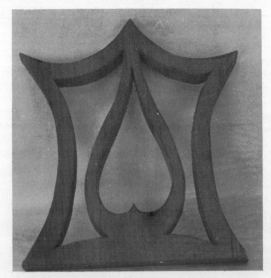

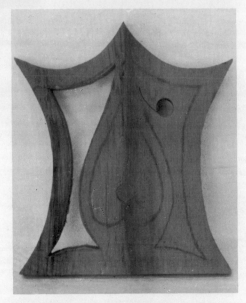

Above left, Fig. 14–6 Finished study for a piercing. Above right, Fig. 14–7 Study piece for another piercing. Right, Fig. 14–8 Study showing part of the process of making a piercing similar to Fig. 14–6.

As you progress in this field of endeavor, you will find that piercings will be required more and more for the decorative value they may add to the finished items.

In the study pieces shown above, the piercings were required to develop the legs of the men figurines and also the Mermaid's arm, as well as the several details of the "Fisherman" carving. The list could be extended but further illustrations would add nothing to the methods involved.

15

Making and Carving
a Bremen Eagle

The name applied to this carving is for identification only.

The dimensions of this piece are—wing spread, 48″; overall height, 15½″; thickness of the body section, 2¼″, rough. The head will project forward 7½″.

One piece of white pine plank is used for the body, wing and tail sections. The head section is made up of two pieces of this same plank glued up with a new adhesive, P.C. 7. It is water-, heat- and wear-proof and if you follow directions on the can, it works perfectly. It can be readily carved.

After applying the glue to the head section blocks, Fig. 15–1, clamp the two parts together and allow them to set for about 24 hours. These parts must be jointed up perfectly for a good glue job. Once the glue is set, remove the clamps and lay down the outlines for the head and body; then bandsaw details out. Fig. 15–2

Left, Fig. 15–1 Head block glued up and clamped. Right, Fig. 15–2 Outline of head is laid out on head block after having clamps removed.

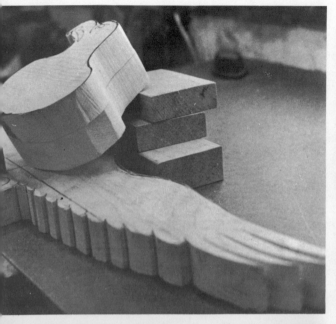

Above left, Fig. 15–3 Head block is placed on body of eagle in the selected attitude and is blocked up. Above right, Fig. 15–4 Shear line being scribed parallel with body of eagle. The dividers are held vertically as they are moved all about the head block. Left, Fig. 15–5 Mitre square being used to determine the angle at which the base of the head block is to be cut on the table saw.

While the glue sets up on the head block, profile out and bost out the wings, the tail and the body section.

After bandsawing the head block, place it in the desired attitude on the body area of the other part of the carving and when it is so located, block up the back part as in Fig. 15–3. Then scribe the line on which the head block is to be sawed out with dividers, Fig. 15–4, and once this is done, saw the head block out on the bench saw, having determined the angle with the mitre square, Fig. 15–5. The table top is set at this angle, of course.

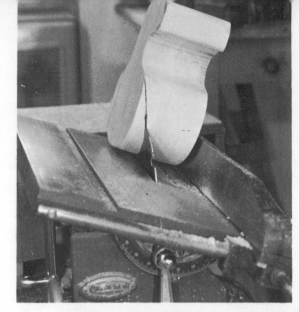

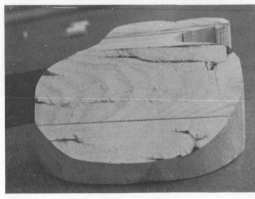
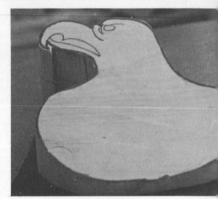

Top left, Fig. 15–6 Table saw top is set at angle and the ripfence set over so that the block can be properly guided. Top right, Fig. 15–7 Head block has been cut on sawtable—saw scarf depth is 2 1/4". Balance of cut has to be sawed off by hand. Bottom left, Fig. 15–8 Shows the completed saw scarfs for head block. Bottom right, Fig. 15–9 Front view of head block after having back trimmed off as in Fig. 15–8 Ready to plane off back.

Then saw out on this line as deeply as you can. In all probability, you will have to finish this sawing with a hand ripsaw. Figs. 15–6, 15–7, 15–8, and 15–9

Joint this base cut up and try it on the wing section.

A good fit must be made between these parts for a successful carving.

Bore three holes about as shown in Fig. 15–10 into the head block with the 1/2" diameter boring tool to a depth so the bottom of the tool stops about an inch above the base cut. Then drill a hole through the stock with a 3/16" drill so three #10 2" wood screws can be used to hold the parts together as work proceeds.

Fig. 15–10 The three screw holes being bored to a depth so that screw heads will be at least 1" above back of block.

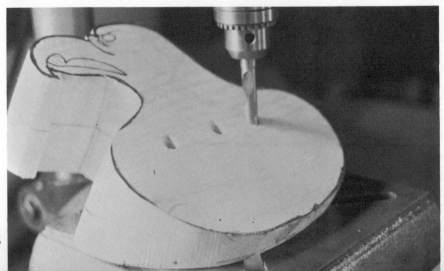

Fig. 15–11 Head block
mounted on swivel jig for
carving and modelling.

A jig made according to the one in Fig. 15–11 can be used to facilitate
the further work on the head block. Mount the block on this jig and bost
out the outlines so further detail can be drawn on the block.

Remove the jig and place the head block on the body section. Set three
screws into the wing section and roughly cut the head block to fit the wing
and body section. Figs. 15–12 through 15–22

Left, Fig. 15–12 Bosting out face of head block. Note the head and beak are
roughly cut to shape. Right, Fig. 15–13 Bosting out back of head and neck
detail.

Top, Fig. 15–14 Second process in bosting out back of head block. Center, Fig. 15–15 Using wood rasp to shape up bosted portion of head and neck. Bottom, Fig. 15–16 Using spokeshave to smooth off rasp marks.

Top, Fig. 15–17 Bandsawing out feather ends of eagle. Center, Fig. 15–18 The body has been completely bandsawed out on design lines. Note that the position of the head block has been heavily outlined; this is to make sure that no carving tools will be used inside this area. Bottom, Fig. 15–19 Head block is placed on body before any bosting has been done on entire part. This enables both the proper attitude of the head to be determined and the outline of the head to be drawn on body of bird.

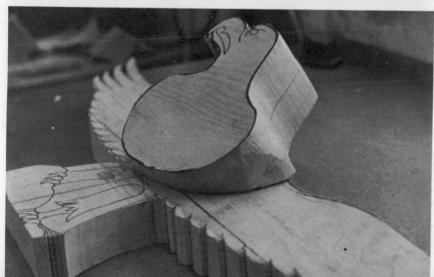

67

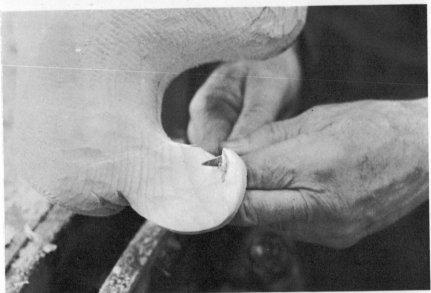

Top, Fig. 15–20 The wings, tail, and head block have been bosted out. The head is held in place by 2″ #12 flat-headed screws. Center, Fig. 15–21 Using riffler to shape up the lower part of the eagle's bill or beak. Right, Fig. 15–22 Both claws have been bosted out, and work is progressing on the eagle's legs with a broad gouge.

Top, Fig. 15–23 The head block and body have been assembled, and the lines for the feathering on both portions have been drawn in. Bottom, Fig. 15–24 The back side of the eagle's head has been limned out as well.

Scribe the feathering out lines on both parts of the carving and remove the head block. Figs. 15–23 and 15–24

Carve in the feathering on both parts as well as the head details. Be sure that you take care as the shape of the beak is developed as well as the detail of the bird's mouth, that is, both parts of the beak. Fig. 15–21

Carve out the eye, the cere and the nostril as well and do this on both sides of the head. Fig. 15–2

Finish carving the details on the wing and tail sections.

Place the head block again on the wing section and check it for fit in all respects. Do not screw it down. The last operations are to finish feathering out the head section except for the details where the two parts are to be jointed up. This pertains to the feathering detail on the body section as well. Run these cuts up to but not past the outline of the head block.

The last operations are these: glue up the two parts, set the three screws in the head block up tight, set the piece aside for the glue to set. Then when this is done, mount the whole thing on the plywood back-up and carve the two parts together as in Fig. 15–20

The last thing to do on the piece, so far as carving is concerned, is to plug up the screw holes, making sure the tops of the plugs project above the head block.

If you set these plugs with Duco cement, you will have to wait a few minutes before you can pare them off; then carve the feather lines across the tops of the plugs and so, complete the Bremen Eagle. Fig 15–25

Do not forget to plug up the screw holes on the back of the wing section where the hold-down screws were put to hold it on the plywood back-up and to provide the means for supporting the eagle on the wall.

I suggest that this carving be gilded. It will take about 4½ books of gold leaf for the job.

The details in carving the wings, the legs, and the tail sections of this eagle have all been described in Chapter 10. The techniques and processes followed will be similar and need no repetition.

Fig. 15–25 The feathering on the eagle has been completed. The carving is complete.

16
Dowels, Wooden Plugs and Dutchmen

Dowels are used when it is desired to hold a compound carving together securely in place of metal woodscrews.

Plugs are used to fill in counter-bored holes on a carving, as in the case of the Bremen Eagle head and body blocks (chapter fifteen). In this case 2" long plugs were used to fill in above the heads of the woodscrews. This is done so the final carving will not show the screw holes, of course.

There are some other uses for plugs as well. For instance, at time a pitch-pocket will show up on a carving that is not evident when the work started. Should this be a small blemish, the place can be counter-bored and a plug inserted to cover over the blemish. This is true when a small knot is uncovered also.

Incidentally, should a blemish develop that is too large to be covered with a plug, a "dutchman" can be used instead. If you will follow the techniques shown in Figs. 16–1 through 16–4, the dutchman can be used

Left, Fig. 16–1 A dutchman ready to inlay over a knot which is being cut out in Fig. 16–2 along the dutchman outline, right.

Fig. 16–4 Waiting for the adhesive to set before planing the dutchman off.

Above, Fig. 16–3 The dutchman is being set into the cut-out portion by tapping it in place with a hammer and plug. Adhesive has been applied to the dutchman and in the hole.

with some degree of success. Set the dutchman in with the same adhesive you use for all parts of a compound carving. There is an exception to this rule—which is that if the blemish to be replaced with the dtuchman is on a carving that is to be finished in natural color and waxed and polished, the dutchman is set in with Duco cement. A word of caution, be sure the dutchman is made of the same stock as the carving and that its grain and color match as closely as possible those of the original piece.

Plugs are cut across the grain of the wood. Fig. 16–5

Dowels are cut along the grain of the wood. Figs. 16–6, 16–7, and 16–8

Right, Fig. 16–5 Plugs have been cut with a plug cutter but are not yet trimmed from the block.

72

Fig. 16–6 The plugs which have been cut free from the block. Saw scarf is noticeable.

Fig. 16–7 A dowel has been cut along the grain of the wood with a plug-dowel cutter.

Fig. 16–8 The completed dowel and the block from which it was cut.

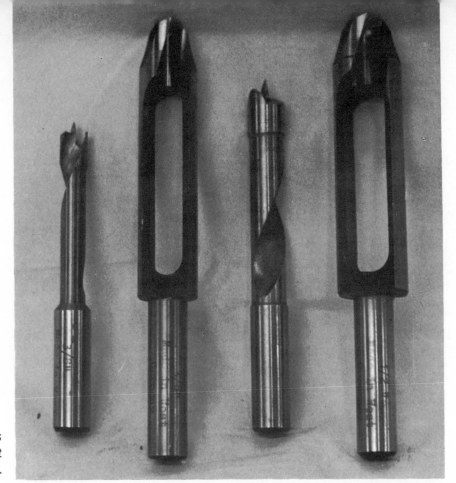

Fig. 16–9 Two different sizes of boring tool—about 3 1/2″ in diameter.

Two sizes of new style plug and dowel cutters are shown in Fig. 16–9, along with the same two sizes of brad-pointed boring tools.

Fig. 16–10 shows the ½″ brad-pointed boring tool about to be used.

There are times when a dutchman has to be fagged-in on a table top or a similar piece of furniture. Unless the piece is to be a very formal thing, the dutchman can be made of wood of a contrasting color and grain.

Fig. 16–10 Brad-pointed boring tool about to be used on a block of wood.

I have, in the past, fagged-in dutchmen made of mahogany, black walnut, teak and red pine on the top of a coffee table. This to make it a "conversation piece."

The term, "fag-in," is an old one used many years ago to describe this process. It is, in reality, applying a piece of veneer to the object so treated.

Once the dutchman adhesive has set, it is necessary to plane or pare off the protruding top of the insert flush with the face of the wood to which it has been applied.

Fig. 16–11 Here is another example of a dutchman. This one has been planed off smooth to the face of the stock. Also shown are two plugs, one pared off and one still projecting above the blemish.

17

Making and Carving
a Laurel Wreath Mirror Frame

There are three tricky problems you will have to solve in making this piece.

First, drawing the outline.
Second, jointing up the parts.
Third, how to bost out the frame.

The frame is basically elliptically shaped, and it can be drawn either by following the mathematical formula for an ellipse, or, if you prefer, it can be drawn freehand. Determine the size you wish to make the piece. Lay down the horizontal line, A-C, and then the vertical intersecting line, B-D. Index the extreme dimensions on these two lines, Fig. 17–1. Index the center, E.

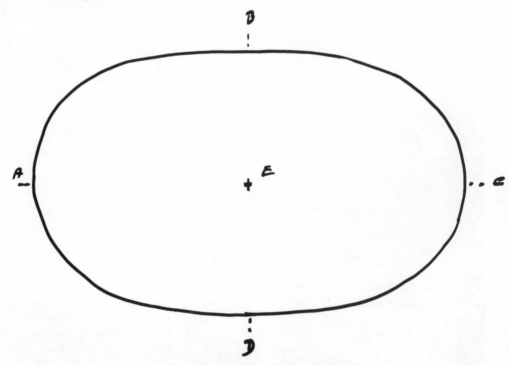

Fig. 17–1 Elliptical shape for frame showing points A-B-C-D-E.

Freehand procedure—use your elbow as the turning point, i.e., center, and swing your pencil so it will make a broad curve, touching both points, A and B. Your first line will look odd, I assure you. Keep on drawing this line until you think it is the curve you want to develop. Trace this line off indexing both points A and B and the center E. Flop the paper over so, in reverse position, point A coincides with point C, and B coincides with point B. Use carbon paper and trace this section of the curve down on the original sheet. Reverse the traced off line by placing point A on C and point B on D and trace that off with carbon paper. Ditto the last section. If the overall design pleases you, there it is; if not, change it until it does by increasing the width. This is the usual procedure for reshaping an ellipse. Fig. 17–2, and 17–3

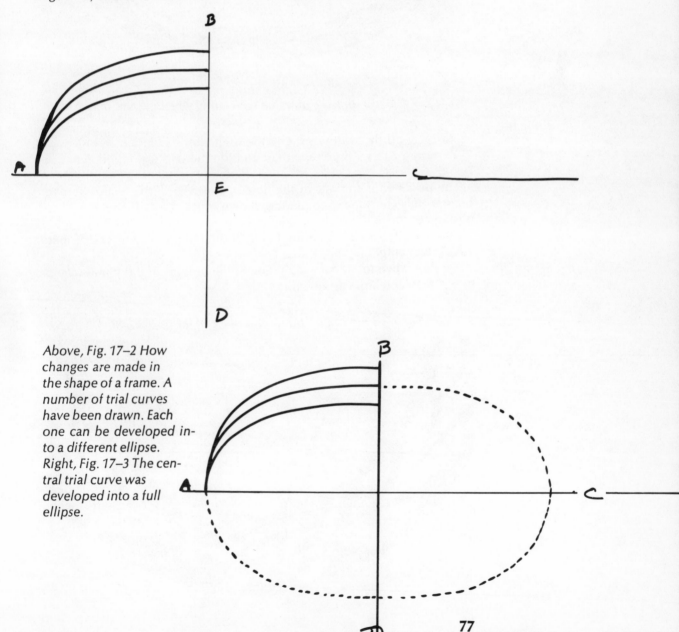

Above, Fig. 17–2 How changes are made in the shape of a frame. A number of trial curves have been drawn. Each one can be developed into a different ellipse. Right, Fig. 17–3 The central trial curve was developed into a full ellipse.

77

Fig. 17–4 Full-size drawing of frame with laurel wreath leaves drawn in.

Next, lay off the width of the frame itself; this dimension to be about 2¼″ more or less. This line is drawn inside the one just laid down. See Fig. 17–8.

The next step is to draw in the details, which in this case are the two branch ends and the facine binding shown in Fig. 17–4. Then lay out the position of the joints at either side of the frame.

The overall dimensions of the frame illustrated are: width, 32″; height, 18½″; branch ends project about 1½″.

An alternative to the facine binding at the bottom of the frame would be a ribbon and bows as shown in Fig. 17–5.

Fig. 17–5 Alternative binding in place of facine binding.

Fig. 17–6 A (top) is the cross-section of the laurel wreath frame.
B (bottom) is the cross-section of the eagle and stars frame (which is to be discussed next).

The cross-section which is to be developed is shown in Fig. 17–6b. Note that the mirror glass reveal is shown; this is ¹/₂″ wide and ³/₈″ deep. The cross section of the frame should be more or less oval in shape, the outside curve extending downward to the back chamfer, which should be about ⁵/₈″ above the bottom of the frame. On the inside of the frame, the side is straight below the downward curve. The reveal makes the difference in this case.

Fig. 17–7 Vertical rendition of a laurel wreath frame.

The following are the necessary steps to follow to make the frame up so it will resemble that shown in Fig. 17–30.

1. Use straight grained, clear white pine plank for the frame.
2. Plank to be at least 10$\frac{1}{2}$" wide. Clip off two pieces, 32$\frac{1}{2}$" long, for the blanks.
3. Use a hollow ground, razor-sharp, combination saw and saw off a piece about $\frac{1}{2}$" wide from one edge of each plank. Be sure the blade is square with the face of the table.
4. Lay out a half joint on one end of one plank. Set ripfence and height of sawblade to make the necessary two cuts, one after another, and saw out the joint. Fig. 17–8
5. Transfer these dimensions exactly off on the second plank and repeat the cuts. These two joints must fit tightly. Clamp the two parts together to see they are tight. Fig. 17–8

Fig. 17–8 Half joints on edges of frame have been sawn out. The design has been laid down on the planks.

6. Plane off both faces of both planks if necessary.
7. Join the two pieces together and clamp in place. Lay off on these two parts the design you have made with carbon paper.
8. Bandsaw out both pieces. Be sure to leave waste-stock.
9. Use spokeshaves and shape up the saw scarfs both inside and outside. Figs. 17--9 through 17–13

Left, Fig. 17–9 Both halves of the frame are bandsawed out inside and outside. This shows the half joint with the waste stock left to be pared off. (Step 8)

Right, Fig. 17–10 Outside of frame has been smoothed up with spokeshave at the half joint. (Step 9)

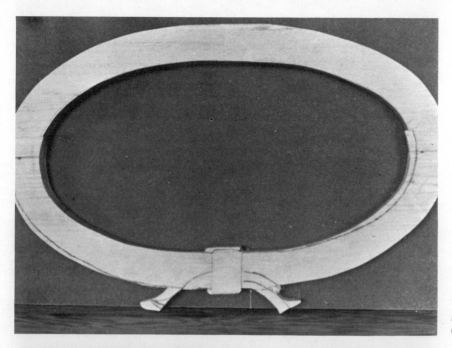

Fig. 17–11 Both sides are joined up to check detail of fit of the half joints.

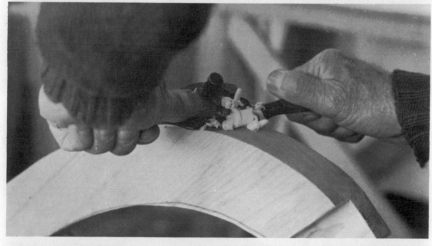

Fig. 17–12 Using a spoke-shave on the end grain. Note the blade is at a skew —the blade is also razor sharp! (Step 9)

Fig. 17–13 Using a spoke-shave to smooth up the inside face of the frame next to the butt for the facine binding. (Step 9)

81

Fig. 17–14 Using a routing cutter as an end mill to develop and rough out reveal for the mirror. (Step 10)

10. Lay out mirror reveal on back of frame. Set up the routing cutter on the drill press, use the hold-over to steady the stock; make this reveal in several light passes across the tool. Do not let this tool take command of the situation; if it does, it will foul things up. When made, smooth this reveal up if necessary. Fig. 17–14

11. Glue up both parts; use *Elmer's Glue* or its equal for this. Clamp the joints up tightly. Let set in a warm place overnight.

12. When ready to work, unclamp joints; use various tools to shape up the frame in the oval shown in Fig. 17–15. I used an inch wide skew chisel to make the rough cuts, then followed this with spokeshaves as shown in Fig. 17–16. If you use the inch skew, take it easy unless you are experienced with this tool. Figs. 17–17, 17–18, and 17–19

Top, Fig. 17–15 With a spokeshave, shaping up outside of oval form for frame. (Step 12)

Bottom, Fig. 17–16 Showing the oval form at the curved end after it has been started to be shaped with a spokeshave. Small progress will be made across the end grain. (Step 12)

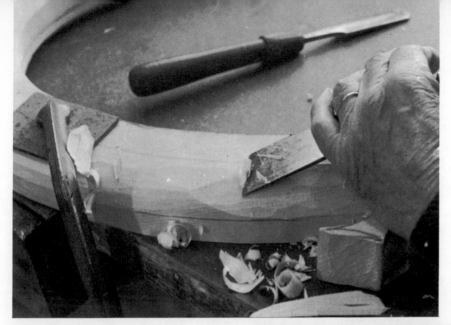

Fig. 17–17, Fig. 17–18, and Fig. 17–19 Showing how the 1" skew chisel is used to bost out the oval form of the frame outside and inside. (Step 12)

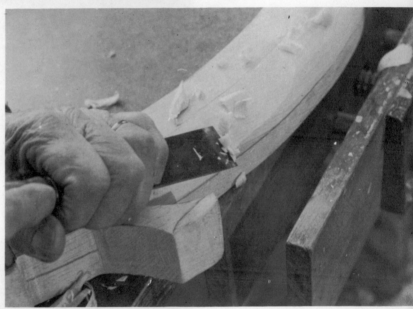

13. Do not bost out the branch ends at this point.
14. As you work on the end grain, take light cuts with all the tools you use.
15. Bost out the facine binding. Fig. 17–20

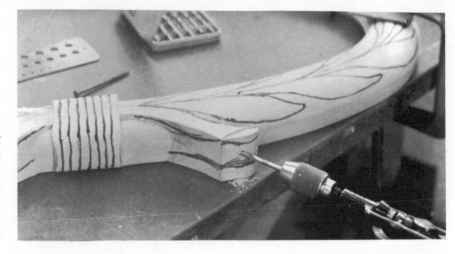

Fig. 17–20 Facine binding butt and the branch ends within the frame outlines have been bosted out. Drilling the hole for pin reinforcement is begun. (Step 17)

16. Bost out the portion of the branches on the face of the frame.
17. Reinforce the branch ends with two metal pins. I used two ten-penny nails whose heads had been cut off with a hacksaw. Using a 5/32″ drill in the hand drill, I bored two holes, one in each branch, exactly in the center of each projection and parallel with the length of the branch, to a depth just under the length of the pin. Then I loaded the hole with Duco cement and drove the nail (pin) home and set it in about a ½″. Fig. 17–21

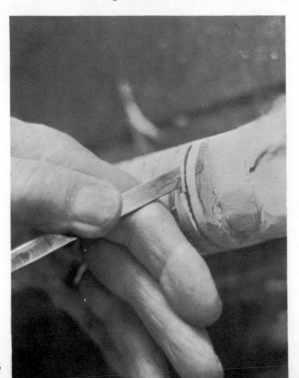

Fig. 17–21 Starting to carve up the facine binding. (Step 18)

Top, Fig. 17–22 Further detail carving being done on facine binding. (Step 18)
Center, Fig. 17–23 Branch ends being bosted out. (Step 19)
Bottom, Fig. 17–24 Facine binding is completed, the carving of the branch ends is finished.

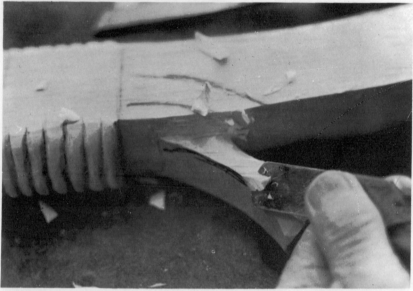

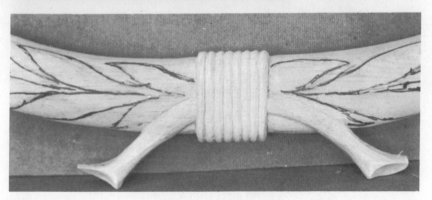

18. Carve up the facine binding. Fig. 17–22
19. Bost out and carve up the now reinforced branch ends. Fig. 17–23 and 17–24

Right, Fig. 17–25 The wreath design has been laid down on the shaped up frame which is now ready for detail carving. (Step 20) Below left, Fig. 17–26 First position of 3/8" skew chisel starting outline cuts on upper section of laurel leaf. (Step 22) Below right, Fig. 17–27 Second position of skew chisel in making outline cuts. (Step 22 continued)

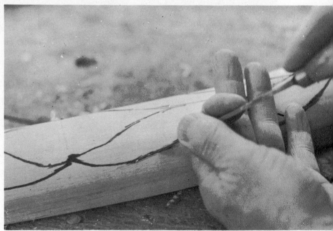

20. Lay down the leaf detail in toto on the shaped up frame. Be sure your design can be carved on these curved surfaces. Fig. 17–25

21. The design must not run below the chamfer on the frame outside nor down to the glass reveal inside.

22. Use a ³/₈" skew chisel and stop cut all about the entire design. Figs. 17–26 and 17–27

23. Back cut to these stop cuts.

24. Repeat these processes until you have made the stop cuts 3/16″ deep all about the design.

25. Use various chisels and gouges to pare off the waste-stock between the leaves and the rim of the frame. Be sure you do not carve below the chamfer on the outside.

26. Using the 5/16″ skew, model a slight chamfer on the edges of the leaves and stems.

27. Draw in and then line out the midrib on each leaf with a veiner.

28. Use fine sandpaper and sand off the entire surface of the frame. Do not sand out all the tool marks.

29. Apply a coat of gesso to all surfaces of the frame, front and back. Be sure you have filled in the nail holes on the branch ends. Fig. 17–28

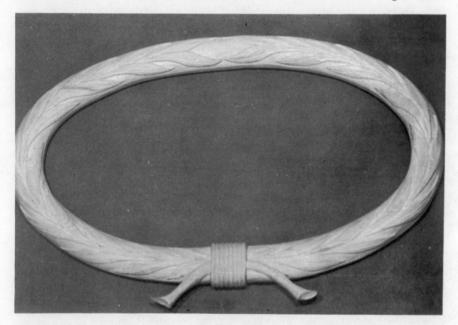

Fig. 17–28 The entire detail for the wreath has been carved, and gesso has been applied to the finished carving. (Step 23 through Step 29)

30. When dry, sand off this gesso and apply another coat.

31. When the second coat of gesso is set, sand that off with fine sandpaper, #220 grit.

32. Set a pair of brass screw eyes on the back of the frame so when the frame is hung on the wall, the wire will not show above the top. Use twisted wire to hang the frame up with.

33. Paint all the surface of the frame, front and back, with two coats of aluminum paint.

Top, Fig. 17–29 The aluminum paint has been applied, and the carved detail has been gilded. (Step 33 and 34) Bottom, Fig. 17–30 Two coats of flat black paint have been applied to the nongilded surfaces of the frame (Step 35) The carving is now completed.

34. Apply gold size to the entire detail carved parts, let set and then gild. Fig. 17–29

35. The day following gilding, paint all the remaining surfaces with two coats of flat black paint. Don't muck up the gilding with this. Fig. 17–30

36. Make a pattern for mirror glass out of untempered hardboard that just fits the reveal nicely. Have the glass cut to this pattern, specify on the checkered side that the opposite face must be nearest the glass.

37. Try the mirror. If it is too tight somewhere, trim off the frame, not the glass. Specify either double thick or crystal glass for the mirror.

38. To fix the mirror in the frame, place it properly in the reveal; then using the hardboard pattern as the back-up and $3/4''$ #16 brads every eight or ten inches about the perifery of the reveal, drive the brads in about half their length.

39. Two weeks after gilding, burnish these surfaces up brightly with a velvet patch. Do not use too much force in this process.

40. Armed with this piece, take it in the house and proudly present it to your wife, if she has not already thrown it out the door.

As you will find out for yourself, working on this piece, it is one of the more difficult problems I have set forth in this book.

18
A Federal Mirror with Eagle, Stars and Scallop Shell

The making of this mirror involves the techniques followed in some of the previous chapters as well as some new ones. The Bremen eagle used to top this piece out is described in Chapter 15; the same techniques described there pertain to this piece as do the techniques described for the rope molding, in part, and also the scallop shell described in Chapter 9. The new procedures involved are these: the curved rope molding at the ends of the frame, the shell carved in the half round, and the manner of making the tangs for the half joints of the frame that are parts of the eagle and the shell. The finished frame is shown in Fig. 18–1.

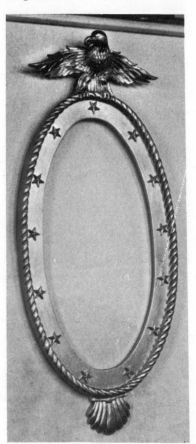

Fig. 18–1 The finished eagle, shell and star frame.

Making the half joints on either ends of the frame sides is also new.

Dimensions of this piece are: wingspread of eagle, 16"; overall height, or length of this piece, 42"; overall width, 19"; width of sides of the frame, 2³/₄"; scallop shell is 4¹/₂" long, outside the frame, by 5¹/₄" wide. Rope molding is ³/₄" thick, by ⁷/₈" wide. Eagle is made from 2" clear white pine plank. Frame and shell are made from ³/₄" thick board, also clear white pine as is the rope molding. The stars are cut from a 1¹/₂" circle, thickness, 5/16", made from mahogany. Pine is too brittle for these.

First step—make your drawing to full scale. Design the outline for the frame freehand as specified and described in the preceding chapter. The procedures to follow to make this piece are—

Trace off the outline of the eagle on the plank, piece to be about 20" long. Also, on the waste stock from one lower corner trace off the outline for the head; be sure you leave some stock for the body block of this part. Be sure you show the tang for the half joints on the bottom of the bird's tail, this part to be not less than 3" long and 3" wide.

The side frames are to be made from an eight foot board planed smoothly on both faces. The edges of this board are to be planed straight and square with the faces also. This board should be 10¹/₂" wide.

Lay the drawing for the frame sides on the board so the ends of each side coincide exactly with the edge of the board. Trace off the outlines for both sides. Clip these two portions off the board and see that they fit each other exactly, or as nearly so as possible at the point where the ends of the side frames are drawn. The reason—the half joint will be developed at those points. Be sure the run of the grain of the wood agrees in both pieces. Bandsaw out each part, both inside and outside.

Use 1" #16 brads and brad the two frame sides together and then, using the spokeshave, smooth these two parts up so the edges and the finished profiles are alike. I suggest the outside be smoothed up first, then check the measurements for the width of the parts and smooth up the inside edges. Check to see if they agree, more or less, with your drawing.

Lay out the two pairs of half joints on the ends of these pieces. This joint is to be 1¹/₂" wide on each end of each piece and ³/₈" deep. Fig. 18–2

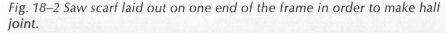

Fig. 18–2 Saw scarf laid out on one end of the frame in order to make half joint.

Make these joints up in the following manner: Set the ripfence of the sawtable over from the outside of the sawblade 1¹/₂″. Set the teeth of the saw up ³/₈″ above the table top. Place the straight end of the joint hard up against the fence and make a cut the width of the frame at that point. Figs. 18–3 through 18–7

Top, Fig. 18–3 "Try piece" for half joint has been half jointed on saw. Center Fig. 18–4 First saw scarf started on end of frame. Bottom, Fig. 18–5 Multiple saw scarfs done on end of frame.

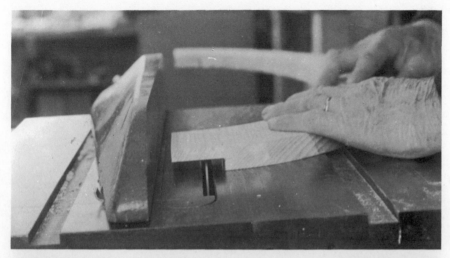

Fig. 18–6 Half joint on one end of side frame completed (gained out).

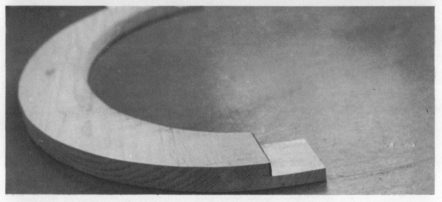

Fig. 18–7 Reverse side frame joint also completed.

Next, make several parallel cuts across the end of the frame similar to the first one made, but between this cut and the edge of the stock; then, slowly and with some considerable care, move the piece across the saw-blade in such manner the sawteeth will shear off the small pieces of stock left between these parallel cuts. This process is tricky. I suggest that if you have never made a cut like this before, you make a study piece and so, learn the technique which you will use again on the other parts. You will, of course, have separated the two parts of the frame.

Follow this procedure on all four ends of the frame.

Next, bandsaw out the eagle and the eagle's head. Be sure of the tang, too, when you do this.

Bandsaw out the scallop shell next.

Next, make the mirror glass reveal ½″ wide, ⅜″ deep in the same way this was done on the laurel wreath frame.

After the four half joints are sawed out, assemble the two sides together with a piece of ⅜″ thick stock, 2″ wide and somewhat longer than the dimension of the frame width, 10″ down from the ends. Brad this temporary piece in place securely. The frame then will become the pattern for the rope moldings and for the completed tangs on the eagle and the shell. Fig. 18–8

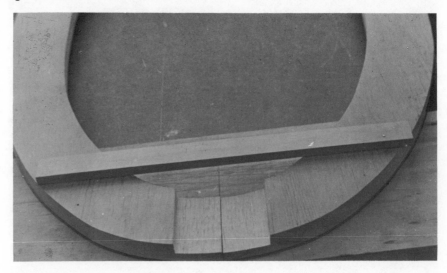

Fig. 18–8 Both side frames held together with temporary stretcher.

Lay out the rope molding in this manner: Put the end of the frame on the ³/₄″ board. See that the edge of the frame almost coincides with the edge of the board. You will need some waste stock at this point. Fig. 18–8

Trace off the outline so that the curve of the frame and the curve of the rope molding will agree. Square the edge of the board up with the center line of the frame. At the point where the edge of the piece of board intersects the frame, make an index mark, one on each side for reference.

Next, trace off the outline for the molding for the sides of the frame on a piece of stock. Be sure you have placed the assembled frame on the board so that the indexed lines from the edge of the top molding board are well within the length of the piece. Fig. 18–9 This shows the end pieces scribed also.

Fig. 18–9 Assembled side frames are laid on stock and side sections of rope molding are scribed.

Bandsaw out the ends and the side pieces for the rope molding.

Smooth up the outside curves with the spokeshave to the finished line. Measure off the width, ⁷/₈″ from the finished curves, and scribe out the inside profile of the molding. Bandsaw these pieces out along these lines, leaving waste stock.

Smooth up the inner faces of the moldings with spokeshaves. This can more easily done if you put them in the vise. Work carefully with the run of the grain on the end pieces. In this case, you will have to constantly shift the position of the piece in the vise. Fig. 18–10

Check these four pieces against the assembled frame sides as in Fig. 18–11. Correct any errors that appear. Fig. 18–12

Left, Fig. 18–10 Smoothing up inside of curved end of molding. Right, Fig. 18–11 Assembled parts are clamped together. Bottom, Fig. 18–12 Checking the pieces for rope molding and scribing the ends of side rope molding pieces.

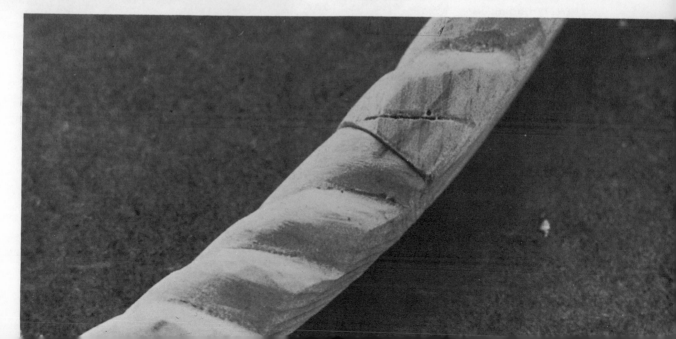

The next step is to develop the tangs on the eagle and the shell. Place the rounded ends of the frame on these two parts; shore up underneath the frame so its bottom will be parallel with the top face of the eagle blank. The shell will have to be shored up to this height above the bench top also. Trace off the curved ends of the frame on both the shell and the bird. Be sure you index the point on the sides of the tangs where the curves intersect these two pieces. Figs. 18–13 and 18–14

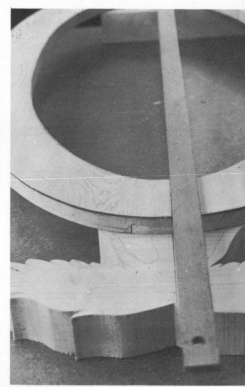

Top left, Fig. 18–13 Assembled parts positioned for indexing side of tangs on bird and shell. Top right, Fig. 18–14 Frame is laid on eagle, and the curve is scribed. Along a straightedge, the center line on all parts. Below, Fig. 18–15 Developing tang on eagle for half joint on sawtable. Note the use of dado cutters for this process.

The surplus stock on both shell and bird tangs will be removed by following the same process by which the half joints on the frame were made. In the case of the eagle, I suggest you use dado cutters in place of a regular sawblade for this. The method is shown in Fig. 18–15. The first cuts for the tangs will be made by setting the ripfence over so the index points just mentioned above are set on the outside of the sawblade, of course.

Keep in mind that this is no place for a careless operator.

Leave a small amount of stock on the faces of the tangs so you can make a good fit when these parts are joined up with the half joints on the frame. This waste stock can be cut away with either coarse sandpaper or rifflers. It is necessary for good work that the back of the tang and the back of the frame fit smoothly together. Trial and error are your guides in this process.

Put the tangs of the eagle and shell into the half joints and scribe curved ends on these pieces.

Before carving the rope molding, fit the tangs on the bird and shell to the half joints. If necessary, smooth off the faces and sides of these two parts for a close fit.

Carve out the curved portions of the tangs to fit the ends of the frame by using a skew chisel for the stop cuts along the line and back cutting with a broad gouge. It will take several series of these cuts to complete this part. When done, or nearly so, check the parts with the frame to show how much more you have to pare off for a tight fit. Then, when done, clamp all these parts, frame sides, shell tang and eagle tang, together. Figs. 18–16 and 18–17

Top, Fig. 18–16 A tang has been developed on the scallop shell. A curve to fit the frame is being back-cut on this part. Bottom, Fig. 18–17 Scallop shell tang is inserted part way into half joint on frame. Shows how the end part of the molding will fit this section as well.

Block the assembly above the bench top so it is level.

Place the end pieces of the rope molding hard up against the curved base on the bird and shell and clamp these parts in place. Be sure they are lined up with the edge of the frame and the ends with the index points on the frame sides.

Place the rope molding for the sides of the frame on top of the curved end parts; scribe a line across the bottom of these where the ends of the curved pieces intersect with the side pieces. Remove these two pieces, square up the lines just drawn on either side of the molding, and with the backsaw, cut off the waste stock at either end. Be sure you leave a slight amount of stock beyond the ends so the pieces can be fitted tightly together.

The fast and easy way to make up these joints is to use a sanding disk on the sawtable and sand the waste stock off little by little until as perfect a fit is obtained as you can make. Make a final check on all the parts: molding, shell, eagle, and frame and see if any further work is required to get them just as they ought to be.

Next, lay out the center lines on the rope molding pieces, first on the center of the tops of the parts, then make the index points on the center lines with the dividers and proceed according to previous instructions, Chapter 12. Be sure that when you draw in the diagonals on the curved end pieces the lines look as if they are almost parallel with one another. They cannot be, of course.

Make the necessary saw cuts along the lines indicating the lay of the rope and, again, following the prior instructions, make the carvings the same way. The trick is to be sure that when you work on the curved portions of the molding you see that the ends of each piece are firmly clamped to the bench top or held securely in the vise.

The reason for this is that you are working across and, not infrequently, against the end grain of the wood. This care is necessary because the wood will fracture if it is not properly secured during the carving processes.

The end piece of molding nearest the eagle cannot be carved where the blocks for the claws are to be glued; a space on either side of the eagle's legs must be left flat for these pieces. These blocks should be 2" long, 7/8" wide, and 5/16" thick. Glue the two small blocks in place.

The processes to follow to model the rope on these curved ends are shown in some detail in the series of illustrations. Figs. 18–18 through 18–23

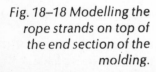

Fig. 18–18 Modelling the rope strands on top of the end section of the molding.

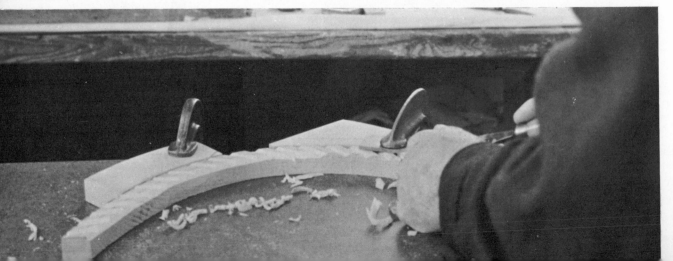

Above, Fig. 18–19 Scribing diagonals for saw scarfs on inside of molding's curved end. Right, Fig. 18–20 End held in vise as backsaw is used to make scarfs on inside face of molding.

Right, Fig. 18–21 Making running cuts on inside of molding along saw scarfs. Note: It is important to see that the tool runs in the direction of the grain. Below left, Fig. 18–22 Second cuts on inside of molding—stock held in vise for this. Below right, Fig. 18–23 Modelling the inside section of curved end. Note how close clamp is to work area.

Do not complete the modelling at the ends of any of the parts. Leave two strands uncarved because it will be necessary to carve these together with the end of the adjacent piece of molding. (This latter operation is shown in Fig. 18–24)

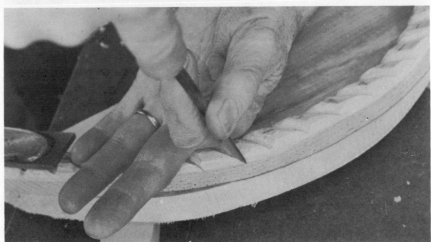

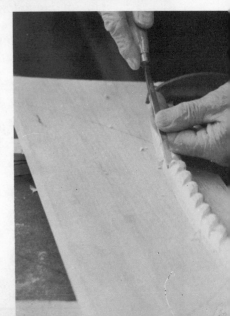

Top, Fig. 18–24 Carving the adjacent ends of each piece of molding together so as to make a continuous border. Center, Fig. 18–25 Carving outside part of curved molding; working with the grain of the wood. Right, Fig. 18–26 Finishing cut on straight section of molding; this finishing cut, like all others in making rope molding, is a rolling cut, tool being slowly rotated to the right as cut is made.

The modelling of the rope lays and strands should be carved about half way down the outside portion of the molding. Make a rolling cut as shown in Figs. 18–25 and 18–26, then carve out the opposite side by reversing the angle of the skew chisel and cutting back toward the inner face of the molding.

Do not, as yet, model the claws. This will be done after the eagle is fully carved, which is the next process. This has been shown and explained fully in Chapter 15 and although the scale is smaller, the same techniques will prevail. Note that the legs will not be fully developed. The lower part will come hard up against the rope molding.

Complete the carving on the eagle and the scallop shell.

Glue up the tangs and the half joints.

Scribe the eagle's claws on the two blocks on the end piece of rope molding by bradding this end piece of molding in its proper position to be sure the claws are correctly located. Fig. 18–27

Top, Fig. 18–27 Blocks glued on curved end piece of molding for eagle's claws. Bottom, Fig. 18–28 End of finishing cut on curved molding.

Finish carving the roping on this piece of stock up to the claw blocks. Fig. 18–28

Carve out the claws. Then carve out the rope molding details under and beside the claw blocks and take considerable care in so doing. This piece of molding will have to be removed from the frame, of course, to make these details.

Fig. 18–29 Ends of two different pieces of rope molding are fitted together as closely as possible. A saw scarf is being made across both parts so as to give the appearance that the rope is a continuous strand.

Once this piece is completed, proceed to carve together the rope details on each end of this piece and the adjacent side pieces.

These parts are to be securely clamped to the bench top when this work is done, Fig. 18–29, and the ends are butted together firmly. You have, presumably, drawn in the necessary guidelines for this work.

When all the carving on the rope is completed, Figs. 18–30 and 18–31, glue it to the frame. I find that you will have good fortune in so doing if you will brad these parts to the frame with 1″ #16 brads after you apply the glue to the bottom of the molding. Don't do what I did once in making this piece. I glued the claws to the shell end, period. I thought it looked a bit odd. Oh well, we all make mistakes.

Top, Fig. 18–30 Carving across the end grain of one piece of molding and into the end grain of the other in order to finish up the modelling. Bottom, Fig. 18–31 The two pieces have been carved together and fitted as nearly as possible. The joint will not show after the various coats of paint have been applied.

Next move is to cut out, carve and assemble the stars on the frame. I suggest you follow these instructions to keep out of trouble—

Make a metal pattern from a piece of zinc, just the size star you want to use.

Use a 5/16" thick piece of mahogany about 5" wide and some 12" to 14" long for the stock for the stars. Pine is too brittle for these pieces.

Trace the outline of several stars on this mahogany; make more tracings than you think you are going to want.

Use a fine-toothed bandsaw and saw out the stars.

Mount three pieces of yellow copy paper end to end, not overlapping, on a piece of plywood ¼" thick, good one face. Elmer's glue is best for this.

When the glue under the paper is dry, spot the back of the stars with the same glue and set them firmly on the paper about two inches apart each way. Let the glue set; then using a very sharp ⅜" skew chisel, carve out the stars.

If, when you are cutting along the grain of the wood on one of the star points, you will make a stop cut at the intersection of the two points, one on either side of this particular point, you will avoid a little trouble with the work's progress.

As each star is completely carved out, use sandpaper and smooth up the carved surfaces.

Lift each star from the yellow paper by placing the edge of the skew chisel underneath the star on the paper and gently pry the two apart. The paper will split. Sand off the remains of the yellow paper on the star's backside and it is ready to mount in place on the frame.

Before you mount the stars in their proper place on the frame, break the sharp inner edge of the frame with #120 sandpaper to a fair radius.

Next, to locate the stars and place them properly on the frame, determine the center of the flat face of the frame between the inner part of the rope and the inner edge of the frame. Use the dividers, measure the location of the center of each star off from your working drawing, center the top star under the eagle and on the center line of the frame, which you have just drawn in with a soft pencil, lightly, and space off each star's center on this line with the dividers.

Mount the stars on the frame by locating them so the center of each one coincides with the center spot on the frame you just made. Apply a dab of glue to each star's bottom part and place it on the frame so two of its points are parallel with the inside face of the rope molding, the opposite point aimed generally at an imaginary center mark inside the frame.

Once the glue under the stars is set, sand off any surplus glue around the edges of the stars.

Check over the entire piece for any irregularities that may have occurred, sand these off, smooth up the entire piece, apply gesso, let that harden, sand that off and then apply three coats of aluminum paint.

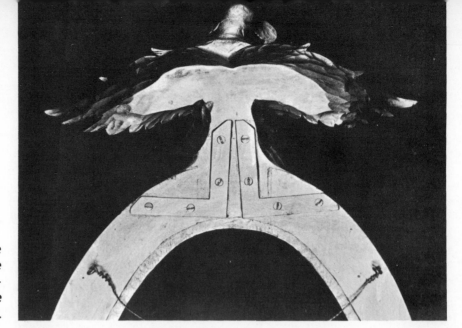

Fig. 18–32 Positioning of the angle irons applied to the back of the frame to reinforce the eagle and the frame.

Provide means for hanging the frame on the wall in such manner that the wire will not show above the top of the frame.

Make a pattern for the mirror glass out of eight inch hardboard.

In the final steps to finish up this carving, the eagle, rope molding, scallop shell and the stars will be gilded. The flat inner face of the frame will be painted flat black; likewise the inner edge of the frame.

The back of the frame should be left painted in aluminum.

To insure that the eagle will always be secure, I suggest that angle irons be screwed in place as I show in Fig. 18–32. The corners of these irons can be filed off or ground off, as the case may be.

Fig. 18–33 An original mirror frame made in 1968. It incorporates an eagle, stars, and a scallop shell in its design.

19
Federal Mirror with Fruit Basket Panel

The photographed of this mirror is shown in Fig. 19–1. The dimensions of the various parts and the overall dimensions are given in the schedule that follows:

Length, overall—33″
Width, overall—16″
Thickness of stock used—³/₄″
Width of frame sides, termed "rails"—2³/₄″
Width of stile, top—3³/₄″
Center separator, width—1¹/₂″
Bottom stile, width—2¹/₄″
Panel full width—10¹/₈″ between rails, overall, 11¹/₈″
Panel depth, i.e., top to bottom, inside stiles—8 1/16″; overall, 9 1/16″

The fruit basket is placed 1¹/₈″ down from the top edge of the panel raising and an equal distance above the bottom of the raising. It is 1¹/₂″ in from the raising edge on either side.

The glass reveal on the back of the frame is ¹/₂″ wide and ³/₈″ deep.

The tenons on the ends of the three stiles, i.e., top, separator and bottom stiles is ¹/₂″. In making these three pieces, be sure you add these tenons to the overall length, not the length shown in the schedule.

Fig. 19–1 A mock-up showing the manner in which the component parts of the frame were clamped together by pipe clamps.

The groove on the inside of the rails is $\frac{1}{2}''$ deep and it is centered on the edge of the piece as exactly as possible. It is made with a set of $\frac{1}{4}''$ dado cutters.

The fruit basket is carved from a piece of white pine stock 7/16" thick and large enough to fit the panel center. Some people may want it slightly larger, some smaller. The choice is yours as to what you think may be the best size to use.

The cove molding used to border this frame is made from $\frac{3}{4}''$ thick pine. It is, as a matter of fact, made exactly the same way that is described in Chapter 12 and one of the side pieces is the piece made to illustrate that chapter, in part.

Three things are important that come to mind in getting the stock out for this frame and that will require some considerable skill.

First, see that the sawtable cutoff guide is exactly at right angles to the sawblade. See that the ripfence is exactly parallel with the sawblade. See that the saw itself is as sharp as it can be made.

The length of the stiles and their tenons must be precisely the same for all three parts. I show in Fig. 19–2 a homemade rig I call a cutoff stop bar. It is, I think, self-explanatory if you will study the illustration. Through its use, the length of stock cut off from longer pieces should be exactly the same, piece after piece.

Left, Fig. 19–2 Cutoff stop bar set to make repetitive cuts of the same length. Right, Fig. 19–3 Shows the use of a holdover and how it is applied to the saw-tabletop.

Another dingus I show a picture of in Fig. 19–3 is a "holdover" that is made of maple and is just thin and flexible enough to allow it to be placed hard up against a piece of stock being machined or grooved or whatever on the sawtable and thus, hold the piece firmly against the ripfence. It is a finger saver. Be sure the end of this clears the saw teeth; otherwise, it may take off across the shop.

The routine to follow in making this frame follows—

1. Make the working drawing to full scale.
2. List off the dimensions of each piece to be used on the mirror frame in their totality.
3. Select out straight grained, clear, smooth, white pine for the material from which the pieces are to be cut.

4. Set up and check the sawtable so the ripfence is in the correct position as has been mentioned. Then set the ripfence up to the width of the side rails and rip them out.

5. Set up ripfence and rip out the three stiles; be sure to check the set-up for proper widths after one edge has ben planed and squared up with the face.

6. Square up one end of each of the pieces you have ripped out on the sawtable. I suggest you use a hollow ground or planer sawblade for the work being done on the table, except for the dado heads.

7. Measure off the exact length of the rails and mark one with the try square at this point.

8. Marry up the sawed ends of these two parts. Clamp them together and then cut them off on the line showing their length. They ought to be exactly the same length. Fig. 19–4

9. Set up the cutoff stop guide to the precise length of the two stiles and the separator; be sure you allow for both tenons in this setup. Put the squared end of each of these parts, in turn, against the hook and make the cuts on all three pieces. Check to see they are the same lengths.

10. Plane off each sawed edge on all the pieces of stock you have thus

Fig. 19–4 Setup for clipping rails of uniform length.

far worked on. Be sure the edges are square with the faces of the parts. Plane the faces on both sides.

11. Make a try piece about half the length of a stile. Square its ends up. Fig. 19–5

Fig. 19–5 Try piece for groove.

12. Set up the sawtable with the ¼″ dado cutters, their height above the table to be ½″.

13. Index, or mark, the exact center of the end of the try piece.

14. Set the ripfence over so that the center line on the end of the try piece coincides with the center of the dado cutters.

15. Make a short cut on the try piece. If this is correct, set the holdover against the try piece and see that the holdover bears hard up on it so it is forced against the ripfence with some pressure. Not so much, however, you cannot move the piece across the dado cutters.

16. Make a full dry run on the try piece.

17. Check the result for accuracy to be sure the groove is centered on the stock and it is the proper depth, i.e., ½″.

18. If the setup checks out, run the side rails across the dado cutters and so, make the groove on each piece.

19. Run off the grooves on the bottom edge of the top stile, both sides of the separator and the top edge of the bottom stile.

20. Remove the dado cutters, replace them with the hollow ground sawblade and set the ripfence over ½″ from the outside of the blade. Set the saw teeth ¼″ above the table top. Follow the procedures shown in Figs. 19–6 through 19–8. These illustrate the method usually followed to make tenons. These cuts and processes have been made before in other pieces in this text. The surfaces of the tenons do not need to be smoothed up.

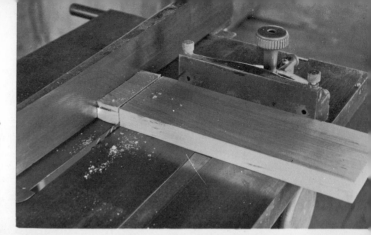

Right, Fig. 19–6 Ripfence set over to the length of the tenon. One cut has been made with the saw set 1/4″ above the table-top. Center, Fig. 19–7 Several multiple cuts are made on both sides of tenon by saw. Bottom, Fig. 19–8 The final cut is being made across the saw to fully develop the tenon.

21. If you have not already done so in getting out the several pieces of stock for this frame, get out the panel next. In so doing, see that the piece is as square as you can make it and that the finished face has been planed smooth and sanded off.

22. Lower the sawblade so the teeth are $\frac{1}{8}''$ above the table top. Set the ripfence over $1\frac{1}{2}''$ from the outside edge of the sawblade.

23. Make a dry run on a piece of waste stock and check the dimensions of this setup.

24. Make cuts across the ends of the panel.

25. Make cuts along the sides of the panel. Figs. 19–9 and 19–10

Top, Fig. 19–9 The second cut is being made along the side of the piece for the panel. The end cuts have already been completed. Bottom, Fig. 19–10 The appearance of the panel after the four saw scarfs have been completed but before any angular cuts are made.

26. Make a try piece, Fig. 19–10, which will be used to set the sawtable at the position to develop the angular cuts for the panel raising.

27. To make this try piece so that the angle of the tapered sides and ends of the panel raising will be developed properly, follow this business—first, make the same cut along the side of the try piece that you just made on the panel face. Draw a line from the center of the piece edge to the bottom of the cut. Fig. 19–11

Left, Fig. 19–11 The try piece showing line of the saw scarf to the bottom edge of the stock. Right, Fig. 19–12 The sawtable has been tilted, and the table has been adjusted so as to make the angular cut to develop the raising of the panel. A "dry run" in part is made on the try piece to check the setup.

28. Run the saw up to about 1½" above the table. Set the ripfence over ³⁄₈" from the outside of the saw. Set the table top at the angle of the line on the end of the try piece by placing this in back of the sawblade and sighting the two together, so to speak. That is, look along the sawblade to see that the angle equals that of the line on the try piece.

29. Make a dry run to make sure the sawblade, the angle and the height of the saw above the table all agree with the try piece. If they don't, make any adjustment required. Fig. 19–12

30. Make the diagonal cuts on each end of the panel stock. Fig. 19–13

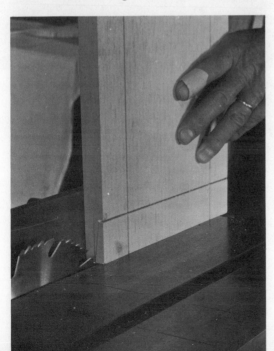

Fig. 19–13 Beginning the angular cut across the end of the panel.

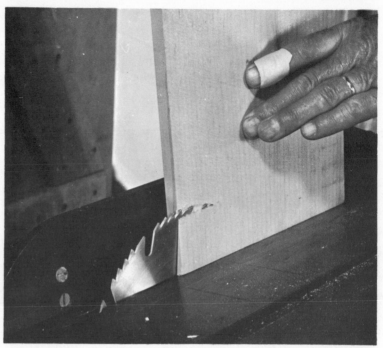

Top left, Fig. 19–14 The angular cut being made along the edge of the panel. Top right, Fig. 19–15 The final angular cut being made on the back of the panel across the end. Left, Fig. 19–16 The final angular cut on the back of the panel is almost completed. Above, Fig. 19–17 Shows the assembled mirror frame.

31. Make the diagonal cuts along each side of the panel. Fig. 19–14

32. Run the sawblade up so it is about 1³/₄″ above the table. Move the ripfence over just enough so when you sight along that and the sawblade when you hold the reverse side of the panel behind the saw, the bottom of the saw will be not more than ¹/₈″ away from the feather edge of the panel, which will be developed as you make cuts shown in Figs. 19–15 and 19–16. A bandaid will help if you just barely touch the saw teeth when the saw was not rotating. Otherwise, it won't be much help.

33. Using a sanding block, sand off any irregularities that may have developed when you made the tapered cuts on the face of the panel.

34. Assemble the various parts together as shown in Fig. 19–17 to see that they fit and that they can be readily assembled with glue a little later on.

35. Take the bottom rail and run the sawblade down so the teeth just clear the underside of the top edge of the groove, Fig. 19–18. Set the fence over so it is ¹/₂″ from the outside of the saw.

Top, Fig. 19–18 Saw teeth are set up to clip bottom edge of groove off. (Step 35) Bottom, Fig. 19–19 Squaring across the table-top at the point where the teeth of the saw start clearing the face of the table. The line where the leading saw teeth clear the face of the table is shown as well.

36. Square up two lines, one on either side of the sawblade where the teeth just clear the table. Fig. 19–19 Draw two black lines along the square to show these positions of the blade.

37. Run the bottom edge of the separator, groove side against the fence, and cut off the edge of the groove. Be sure the finished face of this piece is not on the sawtable top.

38. Repeat this process on the bottom edge of the separator and on the top edge of the bottom stile.

39. Put the bottom stile in its proper place at the end of one of the rails. Draw a line at the edge of the rail where an extension of the line of cut just made (Step 38) to remove the edge of the groove would or does intersect the rail. Square this line down on the outside edge of the rail. Repeat this process with the bottom cut on the separator. These index points show the beginning and end of an "interrupted" cut. Fig. 19–20

Top, Fig. 19–20 Squaring across the back side of the rail in order to locate the index point where the interrupted cut will end. The reverse of this process applies to the bottom of the separator to indicate the point at which the cut starts. Center, Fig. 19–21 Shows the start of an interrupted cut . (Step 40) Bottom, Fig. 19–22 Shows the point at which the interrupted cut stops, that is, the point where the index line for the bottom stile coincides with the leading edge of the sawblade.

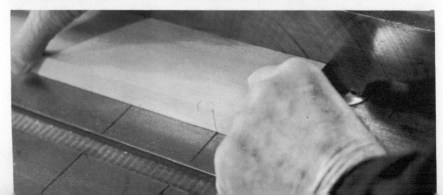

40. This next step is that which is followed to make this "interrupted" cut. With the back of the rail face down on the table top, very carefully lower the piece down on the sawblade so the indexed line on the edge of the rail at which point the bottom of the separator was marked coincides with the dark line on the table top (Step 36), Fig. 19–21, and move the piece slowly along the moving sawblade. Stop the cut when the index line nearest the end of the rail (Step 38) coincides with the dark line nearest you. Fig. 19–22. Reverse the ends of the opposite rail to make this cut on it, of course.

41. Using the backsaw, very carefully cut off the groove edge where the point of intersection of the bottom stile and the rail occurs and make the cut so the saw does not touch the finished inside edge of the rail. Fig. 19–23

Above, Fig. 19–23 Using the backsaw to clip off the bottom of the groove on the rail. (Step 41) Right, Fig. 19–24 All the component parts of the frame being assembled prior to gluing up.

42. A thin web of stock will remain. Clear this out with a skew chisel so the edge of the groove can be removed and by repeating Steps 39, 40 and 41 on the opposite rail, the reveal for the mirror glass will be developed.

43. Assemble all the many parts together so they fit each other and the assembled parts are square with the rails and so, are ready to be glued together. Fig. 19–24

115

44. Disassemble the parts, apply glue to the tenons, the grooves on the rails and the top stile as well as the top of the separator and clamp the assembled parts together.

It is important that this frame be perfectly flat. To assure the glued-up frame is flat, I suggest you use the clamping process shown in Fig. 19–25.

45. A mock-up is shown in Fig. 19–25 of how these clamps are set and how the piece is set up in such manner that when the glue is finally set, the piece will be square and flat, and flatness in such a piece is essential.

In this mock-up, the small clamps are placed so they bear on the pipe below the frame. There is a piece of paper placed between the small blocks of wood under the bottom face of the clamp screw and the joints of the frame. This is so the block will not become glued to the frame at these points. Place paper between the pipe clamp and the joints to prevent the frame from being glued to the pipe, too. The hand clamps are about centered on the top and bottom stiles, horizontally. All four corners of the frame under the pipe clamps are blocked up above the bench top so the hand clamps will not be disturbed or knocked out of line. Figs. 19–25 and 19–26

Fig. 19–25 Mock-up using the pipe clamps and hand clamps. The hand clamps are being used to hold the assembly firmly on the pieces of pipe. Bottom. Fig. 19–26 Close-up view of how the blocks are placed under the pipe clamps to keep the hand clamps clear of the bench.

It is a smart idea to see that the various component parts are placed in their proper relationship, one to another, before the glue sets. I speak from experience, sad and otherwise.

46. Remove the assembled parts from the clamps when the glue has set properly and sand all faces of the parts and joints up smoothly, thus removing any traces of glue that may have been bled from the joints on both sides.

47 Design the fruit basket as you will, making sure that in so doing the piece is appropriately sized to fit the center of the panel. It is impossible to tell just how large or small this decorative piece should be. In the frame shown in these photographs, this basket is 4^1/$_8$″ tall, overall, and 5^1/$_8$″ wide. The basket is about 7/16″ thick at its thickest part. It was profiled out on the bandsaw using a fine toothed blade for the purpose and then, after being sawed out, mounted on a piece of yellow copy paper glued to a piece of hardboard. I used a rather small dab of glue to hold the piece firmly on the hardboard while I modelled the fruit.

Left, Fig. 19–27 The frame is complete except for the basket of fruit in the center of the panel. The cove molding has been applied to the frame. Right, Fig. 19–28 The fruit has been designed and is partially carved out.

Fig. 19–29 The fruit has been glued to the center panel, and the final details which are too fragile to be removed from the paper are being carved.

48. Once this carving is done, make the cove molding for the border on the edge of the frame. This is made in exactly the same way it was shown and described in Chapter 12. In fact, the sample piece made to illustrate this molding in this chapter becomes one of the pieces used on this frame.

49. The molding is mitred together at the corners and is applied to the frame edge with glue and bradded in place while the glue sets up. The brad heads are set below the face of the molding after the glue has set up with a fine nail set and then puttied over.

50. The next step is to apply the fruit basket to the framed panel. Then, once the glue under that part has set, gesso is applied to the whole mirror frame.

51. By the way, the carved fruit basket can be lifted off the yellow copy paper with the same technique used to separate the stars from this same material. You will have to sand off the paper on the back of the carved piece, of course, before it is placed on the panel.

52. Make a hardboard pattern for the mirror glass. Provide screw eyes and wire as the means to hang the mirror on the wall.

53. Apply another coat of gesso to the piece, sand this off very carefully and smoothly; then apply three coats of aluminum paint to the piece and once that has set, apply gilder's size to the entire face and all sides of this frame and when the size is set, gild the piece. Two weeks after gilding, burnish the gold up with velvet and that about does it.

54. I thing the frame will take about four and a half books of gold leaf, and I think, too, it will be worth that much gold.

55. The carving techniques to follow in carving out the fruit basket have all been described and illustrated in some of the preceding chapters and photographs and I think that a description of these in this chapter would be redundant. I shall presume that the use of all the tools needed for this piece has, by now, become very familiar to you.

Fig. 19–30 The complete fruit basket. Two coats of aluminum paint have been applied to the frame. The last step will be to apply one more coat of aluminum paint, then the size, and then the gilding.

20
Stern Transom Carvings for Yachts

Carvings to be used as decorations on the stern transoms of yachts are not too difficult to design, make and apply if demanding attention to detail and some foreknowledge of the difficulties that may be encountered are kept in mind. Figs. 12–18 and 20–1

These transoms are usually crowned, which means they curve outwardly to give the stern of the vessel additional strength. It is this curvature that adds difficulties and interest to the work.

Routine procedures I suggest you follow are these:

Determine what it is that the yacht owner has in mind. Make pencil sketches as you talk with him, if the chance occurs. Settle the probable cost for the work, which will depend upon how much carving he wants done. Settle who is to pay for the yard labor furnished to help you apply the carvings to the transom when this step is ready; also for yard labor in helping you try, fit and take off details. It costs money to travel, to buy stock and for paint and gold leaf. Include these things in your estimate.

A check list of the usual costs in time and of items to be covered in your estimate follow. The times shown are about what it takes me to do the work on each item on a transom about 5½' side to side and 3' deep, i.e., perpendicular.

> Border molding—15 to 20 hours
> Name and hailing port boards—30 hours
> Center decoration, eagle or the like—35 hours
> Mock-up or false transom—labor, 4 hours. Stock cost about $4.00 as of 1973.
> Drawing designs, copying designs, layout—16 to 20 hours
> Mileage—$.10 per mile
> Paint stock and adhesives—$5.00 as of 1973
> Lumber, if pine stock—$45.00 as of 1973
> Lumber, if mahogany—$65.00 as of 1973
> Gold leaf for gilded parts—allow 8 books at market price.
> Fitting time at yard—15 hours

The cost per hour for your time is up to you. If the job is a large involved piece or extensive, I usually charge a little less per hour than if it is a smaller job in time and parts. Once you get to be known as a carver in this field, you do not have to give your time away.

Once these items are agreed upon, proceed as follows:

1. Using heavy building paper, properly named "red rosin," cover the face of the transom with this stock, tape it over the edges so the entire outline of this part can be traced off showing the exact outline.

2. Use a thin piece of pine—I like to use a six-foot pine clapboard for this—hold the thin edge against the center of the transom, use the pencil dividers and take off the curvature of the crown. Have this line sawed off at the yard, try it for fit, and correct any errors.

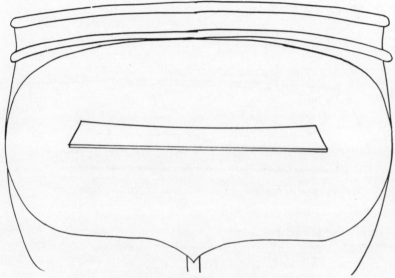

Fig. 20–1 Template of typical stern transom.

3. Make up a false transom by tracing off on wide boards (boards long enough to equal the width of the transom, "athwartships," i.e., from one side of the ship to the other) the curve shown on the profile board. Nail two boards of equal size together, bandsaw out the curve, leaving some waste stock, of course. Shape the curve up to the line with the spokeshave, separate the boards and make stretchers, a pair that will be long enough to span the entire overall width of the mock-up and three or four more that will fit inside the sideboards. Fig. 20–2

Fig. 20–2 Drawing of the mock-up showing how the frame of the mock-up is assembled with the strutters and the two curved sideboards.

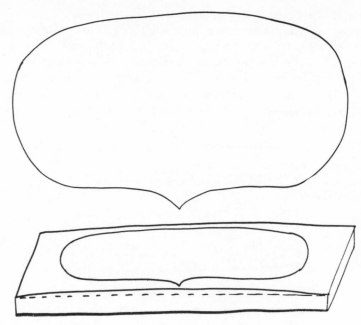

Fig. 20–3 and Fig. 20–4 Outline tracing of the transom.

4. Apply the stretchers to the transom profiled boards for the mock-up, Fig. 20–2, and cover the frame with plywood, good one face. Paint this with two coats of flat white paint. Fig. 20–4

5. Lay the outline tracing for the transom, Fig. 20–3, on the mock-up and use carbon paper under it to trace off the outline of the transom onto the mock-up. Fig. 20–4

6. You would be smart to try the crown pattern on the face of this mock-up just to be sure it is correct. Fig. 20–5

7. Draw in all the details that were discussed with the owner. Fig. 20–6

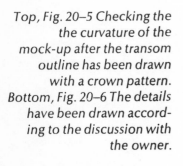

Top, Fig. 20–5 Checking the the curvature of the mock-up after the transom outline has been drawn with a crown pattern. Bottom, Fig. 20–6 The details have been drawn according to the discussion with the owner.

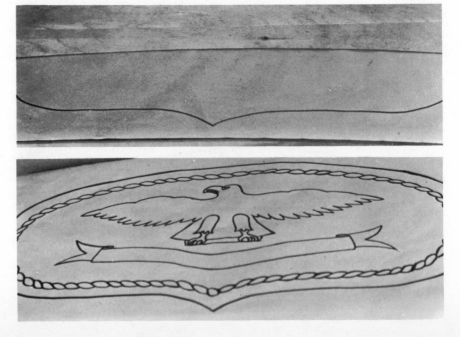

8. Take off the design as laid down and send the drawing to the owner for his acceptance or corrections Fig. 20–7

Fig. 20–7 The design has been traced off from the transom to be sent to the owner.

Once he agrees that is what he wants, follow these steps:

9. Lay a piece of 2″ plank on the face of the mock-up. See if that thickness is sufficient so that you will not have to build up the thickness of the stock. This can be determined if the distance from the ends of the plank, Fig. 20–8, and the top of the mock-up is less than the thickness of the thinnest part of that portion of the design the stock will be used for.

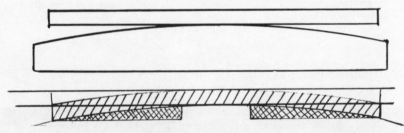

Top, Fig. 20–8 Position of the 2″ plank after it is placed on the mock-up to check to see if additional stock must be added to each end of the plank so that the proper profile curve may be developed. Thickness of the center of the plank must be equal to or greater than the desired thickness of the finished piece. Bottom, Fig. 20–9 Shows how the thickness of the plank can be increased if it is necessary.

10. Fig. 20–9 shows how the thickness at the ends of the plank can be increased and how the final curve can be developed. Glue fillets, if required, with waterproof adhesive.

11.   Lay down the design for each piece on stock suitable in thickness from which the part is to be made. Bandsaw the piece out.

12.   To fit the part to the transom curvature, place the stock in the position on the mock-up it will eventually end up at on the vessel and use the pencil dividers and set them at the distance the underside ends of the piece of stock may be from the face of the mock-up. Then scribe a line along each edge of the piece; and if you will place a weight on the center of the piece being scribed, so the ends are equidistant from the transom, this phase of the job will be simplified, Fig. 20–10. This method of making saw scarfs on the backs of the various pieces is applied to the wings and body sections of the eagle as well—after this piece has been partially blocked out—that is, before the head, wing, feathers and tail section are bandsawed out in detail, thus insuring these parts will not be broken during this process.

Fig. 20–10 Shows the necessity for scribing the curvature of the transom onto the stock from which rope molding or any other part is to be back cut to fit the curve of the transom.

13.   Follow this routine for all the material needed for the parts to complete the entire design. Fig. 20–11

Fig. 20–11 Piece of rope molding with the depth of the back cut indicated by a line drawn on its inside face to show curvature of transom.

14. Make undercuts to remove the necessary material from the underside of these parts in this manner, Fig. 20–12. Use dado cutters to make the saw scarfs with across the material. Be sure the top of the cutters is less than the depth of the cut that is to be made, as well as all the succeeding cuts on either side of the center of the piece.

15. Once these series of scarfs are made, clamp the piece to the bench top and using broad gouges, smooth off the underside of the piece to the curved lines on either side of the piece, lines that were made when you carried out Step 3.

16. Once the bosting and smoothing up of the underside of the parts have been completed, check the pieces against the curvature of the mock-up and correct any errors.

17. In all probability, it will be necessary to make the name and hailing port board as one continuous piece. If this is called for, you will have to make up a joint where these two parts come together. This joint can be made in one of several ways, all of them I have done and they seem to do the job. The easiest is probably the half joint. Fig. 20–13

Fig. 20–12 Dado cutters removing stock from part to be undercut.

Fig. 20–13 Shows how the half joint for the inboard ends of the name board pieces is made.

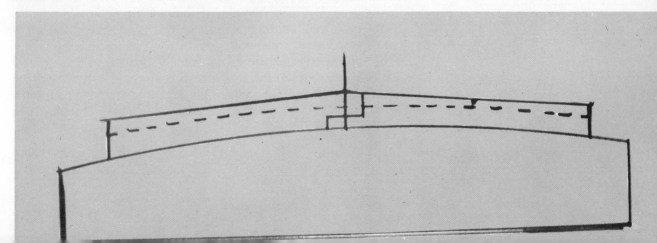

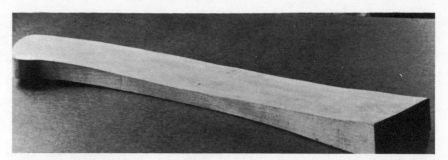

Fig. 20–14 A section of part of a name board that curled so badly it could not be used.

18. In Fig. 20–14, I show a part of a name board that curled so badly from the relief of stress it could not be used. Another piece was made in its place. Note that the top surface of the piece is flat and the straight end square with this face. The joint is made from this flat face on the sawtable.

The important part of this joint is this, Fig. 20–13. The joint is made well above the undercutting for the curvature of the transom. If you do not do this, you've had it.

Refer back to Chapter 17 to refresh your mind on half joints.

19. The half joint overlap on these pieces ought to be not less than four inches. The rough cuts can be made on the bandsaw if you will use a ¹/₂″ wide blade. Be sure, however, the stock does not wind or get twisted as the cuts are made on each piece. Follow the steps shown in Fig. 17–8 and you won't go far wrong. After the joint is made, use suitable wood screws to hold the two parts together as you place the assembly on the mock-up to check its accuracy and fit.

20. Set the pencil dividers at the thickness the piece is to be and scribe a line along the profiled edges, which you should have smoothed up after they came off the bandsaw when you got them out, Step 12.

21. If there is to be a formal end to these pieces, such as a return curve, Fig. 12–18, or a swallowtail, or whatever the design calls for, draw this detail in on the edges of the piece where the variations in thickness or detail may be involved.

22. Should the design call for rope molding about the entire transom as in Fig. 12–18, the steps previously described will pertain except that the pieces must be backcut to fit the curve of the mock-up. This is shown in Figs. 20–9 and 20–12. To make sure the molding does not fracture as you model the roping, make a small false block-up curved so it is similar to the crown curve and use this under the parts being shaped up and carved. Also, use this when you carve the ends of the various pieces of rope molding together, as in Fig. 18–24. The detail of this molding has to be carved on both sides.

23. The eagle used to illustrate this chapter has to be built up in thickness in order to develop the crown profile and have it fit its designed place properly. This can be done in one of two ways, either by adding

stock to the underside of the wings up to the point where the curve will be developed on the underside of the body, or by an overlay for the body on the inner ends of the wings. This last is the more difficult way so I suggest you disregard that possibility. Build up the wing ends instead. To do so, follow the sketches that make up Figs. 20–8 and 20–9.

24. The letters for the name and the hailing port are usually, if not always, incised, that is, carved intaglio. This is slightly tricky.

25. Follow the steps in Figs. 20–15 to 20–18.

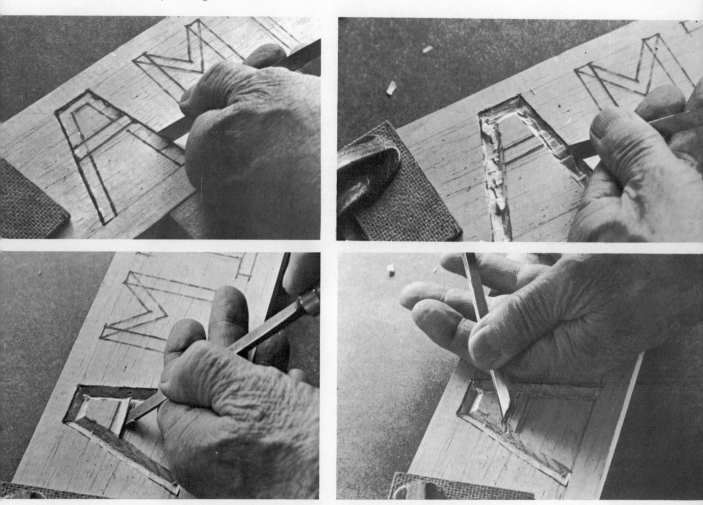

Top left, Fig. 20–15 Using a skew chisel to make first stop cuts for an incised letter. Top right, Fig. 20–16 The outlining of the letters has been completed, and part of the stock has been removed. Bottom left, Fig. 20–17 The incised cuts in the top and sides of the letter "A" have been completed. The bar is being removed. Bottom right, Fig. 20–18 The second step in removing the bar in the letter "A."

Be sure that each part for the transom carvings fit the mock-up properly and tightly, or as tightly as you can make them. There is slight room for error in this.

26.   Once all the parts are completed, finish them up according to the specifications agreed upon when you made the dicker for the work with the owner. All these details have been described in prior chapters. The difference in doing this work and that on other pieces is that you will be using marine paints and finishes all requiring slightly different techniques and all well described and specified on the tins or containers. If you follow these directions, I don't think you can go far astray. Be sure the backs of all your carvings are painted with wear and weather resistant paint stock.

27.   When gilding a marine carving, be sure you use slowset oil gold size. This works best for the exposures the gilding will be subjected to after the vessel is launched and under way.

28.   When you have completed the various parts, check them against the mock-up for fit, take them to the yard or wherever the hull of the yacht is and check them against the true transom. Do this before you apply the finish called for.

I make it a habit to take certain tools with me when I have this sort of work to do and if changes have to be made in the back cutting or the fit of the pieces, I make them at the yard, rechecking the part to be sure it is fitting as it should.

By being forewarned, you can approach your first transom job with some assurance the work will come out as it is supposed to. If you will keep some of the things I have tried to outline in mind, don't let the prospect throw you. Tackle the job and get all the fun you can from such a challenge to your skills and efforts. Good luck.

21
Trailboards

Decorations for the bows of ships have been used for thousands of years—some records go back to 2500 B.C. Men have always been proud of their vessels and that perhaps is why any vessel larger than a row-dory (a State of Maine name for that king of small boats) is always called "She."

The trailboard is used to decorate the bow of a vessel, one on either side, usually just under the foredeck on yachts and under the forecastle-head on larger ones. In Figs. 21–1, I show the trailboards I carved for the "SEA TOY," a ketch owned by Mr. Jay R. Rhoads, Jr. and built for him by Morse Boatbuilding Company in Thomaston, Maine.

Two designs were made for these pieces, one much more elaborate than the other. The simpler design was the one selected.

Once again the process is described in the series of steps, now a routine thing, that I suggest be followed if you are to undertake work of this sort.

1. Make a paper pattern of the actual trailboard. Lay down the design, back the finish drawing up on the reverse side of the pattern with carbon paper, reversed so the carbon side is on the paper rather than the bench

Fig. 21–1 The ketch "SEA TOY", just launched, is about to be hauled into the fitting out berth. The trailboard is shown just below the sail under the figure of the man squatting down on the foredeck.

top, and outline the design on that side of the pattern. Then place the pattern on the trailboard and trace off the design in the usual manner.

The trailboards are almost always made by the yacht yard so there is no need for you to undertake this part of the work. By the way, settle the costs involved for your part of the work as you did in making stern transom carvings.

2. Once the design is laid down on one board, reverse the pattern and trace it off on the opposite one.

3. Darken the lines on the face of the board. Correct or redraw any portion that is not clearly defined.

4. Make stop cuts all about the outlines of all parts of the design with the $^3/_8''$ skew chisel held almost vertically, but canted or tipped slightly outward. Do not make these cuts deeper than 1/16". Fig. 21–2

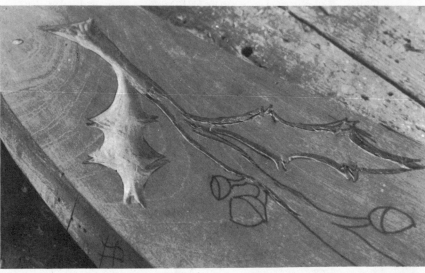

Fig. 21–2 The design has been traced off on the port trailboard, the lines have been darkened, and the first series of stop cuts and back cuts have been made. The branch end and the first leaf have been bosted out with the half inch gouge; back cuts are made on the second leaf outline to the stop cuts.

5. Use a $^1/_2''$ #3 gouge to bost out the stock after you have made the back cuts to the stop cuts. Depth of finished face should be about $^1/_4''$ at the deepest part.

As the work is carved intaglio, you will have to use much more skill to develop the profiles of the various details than would be the case were it carved as relievo.

6. The indentations on the leaf ends will give some trouble if you try to use anything but a very narrow #3 gouge for this bit. These tools are hard to come by, so I suggest these details be developed by using a $^1/_4''$ skew chisel and cut with a winding cut to make the detail. Note the correction made in Fig. 21–3 where the indentations come too close to the edge of the trailboard. This happens not infrequently.

7. In Fig. 21–4, the half inch gouge is used to bost out and carve the detail to develop the acorn.

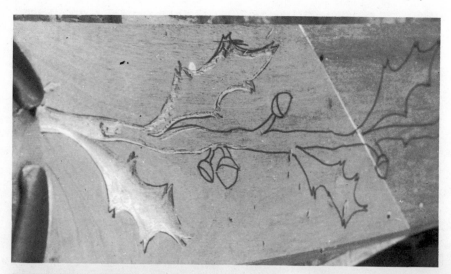

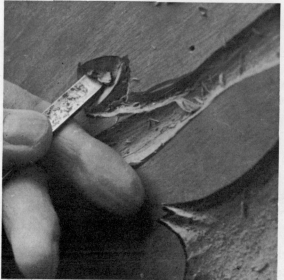

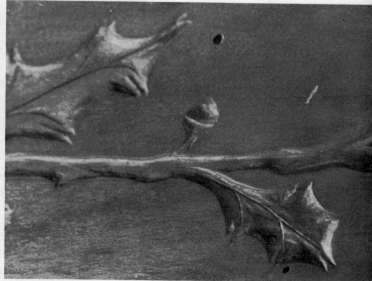

Top, Fig. 21–3 Detail of the branch end. The first leaf is bosted out and the stop and back cuts are made on the second leaf. Note that the drawing has been corrected on part of the second leaf indentations. These were too close to the edge of the board as originally laid down. Bottom left, Fig. 21–4 Detail, bosting out after stop cutting around acorn. Note how the cap of the acorn is developed. Bottom right, Fig. 21–5 The acorn is fully carved and finished. Veining on one leaf has been completed with a parting tool. The veins are drawn in on the leaf in the upper part of the illustration.

8. Fig. 21–5 shows the acorn completely carved and detailed out; the veining on one leaf has been completed with a parting tool; the leaf in the upper part of the picture has the veining drawn in ready to be carved.

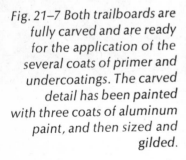

Fig. 21–6 All the detailed finished carvings have been completed on this trailboard. This illustration shows a section of the completed piece near the forward end of the board.

9. Fig. 21–6. All the finished carving has been completed on this trailboard and a section of the finished piece is shown. This picture shows some of the detail near the forward end of the port trailboard. After all the bosting and finished carving is done, use #150 grit sandpaper and sand off, very lightly, the irregularities that may be too prominent when the trailboards are tilted toward the light source. Do not oversand the pieces, however.

Fig. 21–7. Both trailboards are completely carved in detail. The pieces have been given one coat of aluminum paint, except for the carving which has had three coats of aluminum paint. Then the carvings have been sized and the last step, that of gilding the detail, has been done.

Fig. 21–7 Both trailboards are fully carved and are ready for the application of the several coats of primer and undercoatings. The carved detail has been painted with three coats of aluminum paint, and then sized and gilded.

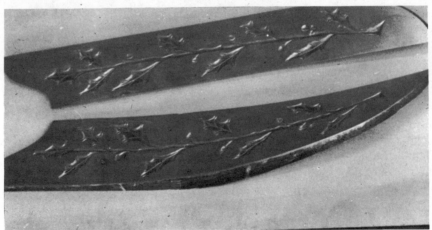

Fig. 21–8 Photograph of an eagle used on one of a pair of trailboards on the motor yacht "LITTLE BITT IV." Pictured is the carving for the starboard trailboard. Both pieces were made from two 2 1/4" pieces of Honduras mahogany plank about 4 1/2" long and 12" wide that were glued together. The back of the carvings were bandsawed and fitted to either bow of the yacht.

These carved pieces were returned to the yacht yard in Thomaston where they were installed on either side of the bow of the "SEA TOY."

After the trailboards were installed, the yard applied the coats of color stock to them; then the teakwood borders were set in place as well as was the teak fiddlehead shown in Fig. 22–3 and Fig. 22–4.

22
Fiddleheads and Billetheads

Fiddleheads are used on various of the sailing kinds of yachts rather than on power boats to finish off the stem piece, or a set of trailboards. They are placed directly under the bowsprit and on the top end of the stem piece. The stem piece is a more or less vertical timber shaped up and tapered as the actual bow piece on these vessels.

The yacht builder will in almost every case get out the stock and make up the fiddlehead to fit the hull but that is as far as his work goes. The final design and its execution will be left to the knowledge and skills of the woodcarver. The blank for this part will be of sufficient width and diameter so the details of the spiral and spire can be fully carved on both sides, port and starboard.

The yacht designer or naval architect may show in some degree what he has in mind when he drafts up the plans for the details of the bow structure, and if these do not agree with the ideas of the carver, it is a wise man who asks questions. I suggest the design be determined beforehand if it is partially shown on the working drawings.

Billetheads are much more elaborate carvings and today, because of high yard costs and the difficulties of maintenance, are seldom if ever used. In the beautiful book entitled *Treasury of American Design,* Volume 1, Chapter 2, pages 46 and 47, detailed paintings of early carved billetheads are shown in great detail and beauty. If such are specified for the work to be done, I suggest these illustrations be studied at some length. I doubt if, in a work of this sort, a beginning woodcarver would want to undertake a piece of this nature so, I will elaborate on how a more simple piece, the fiddlehead, can be designed and carved.

Fig. 22–1 Study for fiddlehead used on 58-foot sloop. Projecting leg fitted against end of trailboard trim.

The several illustrations in this chapter show three fiddlehead studies and one actual fiddlehead carved from teak. The study piece for this one has unfortunately been lost.

In my experience in making up these parts, a study piece is an almost absolute necessity. By making it before you start on the finished piece, all the errors can be made and, hopefully, ironed out.

The carving shown in Fig. 22–1 is that used on a 58-foot sloop. The leg was part of the top molding or border for the trailboards I carved for this vessel.

Fig. 22–2 shows another fiddlehead used on the ketch "WINDSONG," long since built and sold for cruising in the Mediterranean. The vessel was about 60 feet overall. The fiddlehead was used to finish off her stem piece.

Fig. 22–2 Study block for ketch "WINDSONG." Right, Fig. 22–3 Actual fiddlehead. Shows spire on starboard side of this piece. Port side spire was carved on a similar but opposite "twist" or spiral form.

Fig. 22–3 is the starboard carving made for the yacht "SEA TOY" described in the foregoing chapter on trailboards. The port fiddlehead being the carving reverse of this part. The piece was carved in teak.

Fig. 22–4 Study piece to illustrate how fiddlehead is carved as well as designed.

In Fig. 22–4, I show how a fiddlehead is drawn out, how the part is made to fit the trailboards and why a study piece is made so errors can be avoided on the final carving.

The details of this carving are lettered to begin with and the letters indicate the following facts:

A. Thickness of the ends of the trailboards to which this was fitted.

B. Portion of the spire that must be developed to fit flush with the trailboards.

C. Height of the spire, or the "apex."

The leg projecting from the side of this study block will be pared off to exactly fit the thickness of the trailboard rim molding.

To design and make this piece, I suggest these steps:

Make a tracing on paper of the outline of the piece made by the yacht builder and furnished to you.

Work out the whorls or volutes which are to be carved in order for the spire to be developed. The apex, "G," is the true center of the circular outline of the piece.

To draw the whorls, follow this idea—each curved part must seem to be equidistant from the portion of the curve between it and the apex, but actually the diameter is ever-increasing. This is not the easiest design to draw. Expect to take a great deal of time and care in order to develop the final curves or whorls. I cannot find in my books a formula from which this design can be made, unfortunately. It has to be done freehand and worked on until it looks correct to you.

Once the design seems to be correct, trace it off with carbon paper on both sides of the block, reverse the drawing in the same way the reverse drawing was made for the trailboards.

Start the carving at the apex; outline each part of each whorl with ¼″ skew chisel.

Back cut to these outline cuts. Be extremely careful when you make the first back cuts at the apex or that detail will be lost.

Use a #3 straight gouge to develop the planes on each part of each whorl. Use care that you make light cuts in this process because the next step is to use variously sized skew chisels to pare off the surface of each of these whorls into a flat plane.

Stop cut about each raising—I think that is the best term I can use to explain how the spire is finally developed. Each stop cut about the outline of each whorl must be made progressively deeper, but not so deep that the back cutting that must be done will distort the face of the whorl.

In Figs. 22–5 to 22–10, these steps and carving processes are shown in some detail, much more so than I can describe them in words.

The three tricky parts of these things are the apex development, the carving and smoothing up of the point where the piece will be fitted to the trailboard ("B" in the schedule), and the last is the juncture of the whorl and the inside of the border. The point of no return, I guess is the best definition of this.

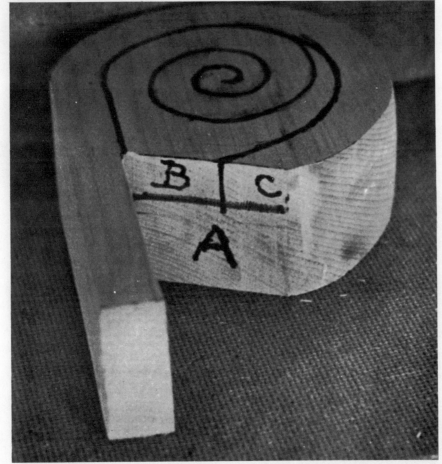

Fig. 22–5 Side view of study piece for a fiddlehead. "A"—Base of carving when piece is completed. "B"—Spiral ends at this point—flush with face of trailboards. "C"—Outer rim of fiddlehead when spire is completed.

Above, Fig. 22–6 Stop cuts around spire made, and first back cuts started. Right, Fig. 22–7 Start of paring cuts on spire. NOTE: First cut starts at tip of spire. Make this first cut carefully! Below, Fig. 22–8 Carving of spire is nearly completed. Note, too, "point of no return" is completed.

Above, Fig. 22–9 Shows the finishing up of the outer part of the spire to the "point of no return." Left, Fig. 22–10 Shows the completed study block.

Variously sized skew chisels will be used to make sure the surfaces of each portion of each whorl is carved perfectly flat, or at least as flat as it can be made by hand.

Note that each part of each whorl is progressively deeper than the preceding part. No easy trick to develop first time out, hence the study piece or pieces.

Once completely carved out, lightly sand off any evident irregularities that you cannot carve out with the gouges or skews.

If you will use a ½" #3 gouge to do this work and to use in back cutting, the work can be more easily done, perhaps than if the skew chisel is used for these cuts. That is a matter of preference, not instruction.

All your acquired skills and knowledge of the use of the tools involved in this piece are required and it is not the easiest thing in the world to either design or carve, but the satisfaction of having it come out properly will pay you great dividends in pleasure.

Fig. 22–11 Study for mermaid figure—head mounted on formalized billethead.

23
Mixing Stains
for Your Carvings

Numbers of people use commercial stains for finishing off carvings for the reason, probably, they have never experimented with dry color stock and linseed oil cut with turpentine. Commercial stains save time and effort but sometimes the results are far from being what the woodcarver had in mind.

The process of making your own color stock for staining is not at all complicated provided you know what you are trying to do and what to avoid.

These are the steps to take to make up this material and how it is used as well as the way in which the color is added.

Dry colors come in several tones and are or at least ought to be readily available in a good paint store. They are sold by the pound. They are as their name implies, dry powder, and so, when you get them home, put them in glass jars and use the usual jar rubber to seal them off from moisture. Buy only those colors that will be of use, namely, Van Dyke brown, raw sienna, burnt sienna, yellow ochre, Indian red, burnt amber; but for goodness sake stay away from chrome and cadmium yellows for use as stain color. Otherwise, the results will be alarming.

The vehicle for these stain colors is linseed oil. I suggest you use raw linseed oil, let down in gum turpentine and when it is ready to mix with color, add a very small quantity of Japan dryer. The proportions for the oil turps mix—one part of gum turps to six parts of linseed oil. One teaspoonful of Japan dryer to four ounces of the oil mixture ought to be sufficient to complete the oxidizing of the oil.

I do not recommend the use of boiled linseed oil for use as the vehicle for staining; it will stay tacky for some time after it is applied.

Keep the oil turps mixture in a tightly capped bottle; make up about a pint of this combination at a time, it will keep if sealed.

To use this combination do the following:

Select a piece of scrap from the wood from which the carving to be stained was made. See that the color of the sample closely matches the parent piece. See that it is finished in the same manner. That is, smoothed up and similar to the piece from which it came.

It does not take too much material to go a long way in this process. Pour off a small amount of the oil mixture in a small glass jar. I find the glass jars that cocktail olives come in are just right for this. Add the dryer, add very carefully the color stock, i.e., dry color, you think will develop the tone you wish to use. Suppose that the piece is carved from Honduras mahogany and you want to darken it slightly more than would be the result if just plain uncolored linseed oil was applied. If so, add a dight of Van Dyke brown. Stir well, put the jar cap on tightly and give it a good long shaking until the color and the oils are blended. Use a small brush or the corner of a cloth dipped in this mixture and wipe it on the try piece. If the tone is too dark, add a bit more oil. If you want to make a radical change in the color from that of the natural wood, try using the Indian red or yellow ochre dry color and see what happens.

Experiment with this business and learn how the various woods react to this unseemly treatment.

A few comments on how some woods do react—white pine will turn on the yellow side if linseed oil alone is applied to it. It will drink in color way beyond your expectations. On the other hand, black walnut will turn dark under oil alone and no matter what other color may be added to the oils, it simply mucks up the looks of the piece. The oil, by the way, will act as its own filler when applied to the carving. You do not need to use shellac or varnish fillers if you will stick to linseed oil.

Mahogany will turn slightly darker as oil is applied to the surface of the finished piece. This holds true what ever kind of mahogany is used. Let me say that neither African (so-called) mahogany or Philippine (so-called mahogany) is true mahogany. It resembles true mahogany but is slightly different both in grain structure and in its general characteristics. These woods can be stained to resemble true mahogany, that is, either Santo Domingo or Honduras mahogany.

Yellow birch is, as its name implies, yellowish light brown in its original state and judicious application of Van Dyke brown and/or burnt sienna will change its tone conspicuoously, so use very little color on it.

Teak need only be oiled to bring out the lovely grain of this wood and if you do oil it, do it with very little oil let down in an equal amount of turpentine. Once applied, wait a day or two, then polish the piece up with a soft cloth.

To apply this homemade stain, use a soft padded cloth. Wipe the oil and color on the piece, take care that you get all the wood oiled up, wait a short time, perhaps half an hour before you wipe off the excess oil.

Before you apply color stock to a piece of furniture for instance, the top of a mahogany table, do follow these steps:

First, see that the wood is clean, has no sanding or tool marks evident and that it is dust free. Let down your oil turpentine mixture with an additional amount of turpentine, about equal to one part turps to three parts oil. Wipe this in briskly with the cloth pad. Let it dry, which will take two days or so, depending upon the weather. Use a pad of four ought steel wool, or #200 grit sandpaper and go over the surface until it is free from the gummy feel that will be evident.

Mix up the color you want to use, the browns, very little of it, however, in the oil turpentine mix in the bottle. Add the Japan dryer, apply this to a corner of the tabletop to see if the color is what you have in mind. If so, apply the oil-color mix to the entire table top. Rub it in briskly. Let it dry, about two days.

Wet down about three tablespoonfuls of finely ground pumice with some mineral oil, enough to make a thin paste.

Put some of this compound on the palms of your hands and then rub the stuff on the table top, all over; keep your hands well covered with the pumice mix and keep on rubbing until the surface is finished up in a soft gloss. Wash the pumice off with warm water and Ivory soapsuds.

Apply a thinned out coat of spar varnish, half turps and half spar varnish to the table top. Let that set. Rub it off with more of the pumice mineral oil mixture until it seems to ball up as you work on the top. Wash that off with soap and water. Dry it with a soft cloth.

Apply varnish in which no other material is mixed, let that dry, rub that coat down with pumice and oil and then—excepting boiling water or hot iron—you can, within the bounds of reason, spill, put or place anything on the table top with reasonable assurance not a thing will happen.

To finally finish off a carving which has been stained, apply hard wax, preferably a natural wax similar to or equal to Butcher's wax, and when that dries polish the piece up with a soft cloth. Apply the wax to the piece about once a year for three or four times and then leave it alone. It will glow, as you will, with pride.

24
How and When to Use Gesso

Gesso is used on carvings that are going to be used indoors as a means of developing a smooth hard background for the kind of finish that is to be applied to the carved piece. This finish may be either polychrome or gilded as the case may be.

Gesso can usually be bought from any art supply dealer. It comes in handy sized cans of various weights and may be either dry or wet as you elect. Wet gesso is a semi-liquid paste and is readily applied with an artist's firm bristle brush. Hair brushes are too soft for the stock.

Gesso is usually made of a combination of marble dust and whiting in a suitable binder. Most gesso now is held in suspension in an acrylic polymer medium. Should you so desire, the stock may be tinted with color suitable to your needs, using a paint stock made of the same stuff as the suspension medium.

Commercial gesso is much to be desired over the homemade variety. If you must be a purist and do it the hard way, you have to mess around with dried animal glue, hot water baths, fine whiting and a hotplate. It is messy and to my mind most unsatisfactory. I have made it and I shall not do so in the future. Better throw it out the door.

Once applied, commercial gesso can be lightly sanded off with fine paper, #220 grit by preference. This does not destroy the "tooth" that good gesso develops to hold paint stock.

Two coats of gesso should be sufficient to fill all the pores of the wood and to develop the hard under surface so desired of the piece to be gilded and burnished to a bright finish. Gesso may be painted over with either the acrylic paints now readily available or with oil tube color stock as you prefer. I suggest you do not use water color stock or casein paints for polychroming.

In event the piece is to be gilded, you can use either quick set synthetic size or the slower oil gold size as the vehicle to which to apply the gold leaf to the carving. Egg white, the old classic size, does not work too well on the gesso just described above.

Should it be that there are fine lines carved on the piece, it may be necessary to thin out commercial gesso with water to a more liquid state than that in the can so the lines will not be filled in.

Should this happen, recarve these lines with a proper tool or use a sanding point or fine riffler to clear them. If a carving tool is used, it will have to be resharpened afterwards because the gesso will dull its ege.

Do not use gesso in any form for carvings that are to be used out of doors. Undercoating on these pieces can best be developed by using three or four coats of aluminum paint, each one lightly sanded down to the desired smoothness, except for the last coat. This will give a high glossy undercoat for the gilding size and the finish, after gilding will be bright.

Whenever gesso is to be used, be careful that brush marks are eliminated through the sanding process on the last coat. I suggest that if one or more coats are used, the second and succeeding coats be cross brushed, i.e., one coat painted on in one direction, the next in the opposite direction. This assures more and better coverage.

25
Use of Color
on Polychromed Carvings

Polychroming a carving involves the use of color stock, the preparation of the background for the color stock and some small knowledge of the business. I suggest that some experimentation be undertaken before the carving is painted up.

This sage idea is based upon my own ineptitude of some years standing.

The problem can be complicated and the best way to find out what it is you propose to do is to make a tracing from your working drawing and use that as the means to work out the color scheme. Once this is done to your satisfaction, follow the scheme out on the carved panel.

The following comments may be of some help.

The routine steps in this endeavor are these:

Make the drawing of the carving, then lay it out on the panel. Next, make the carving. Complete the carving to the point where the background undercoating material is to be applied.

Be sure the undercoating material is the proper stock for the kind of color stock you propose to use. For instance, for indoor use, use commercial gesso. For outdoor use where oil colors are to be used, use white undercoating material oil base. For enamel paint, use enamel undercoating.

If the carving is to be used indoors and gesso is applied as the sealer-filler, you can use either the acrylic polymer paints or artist's oil tube color stock.

I find the best tools to use with the acrylics are the various shapes of brushes made from nylon. Hair or sable brushes are too soft.

After being used, be sure that the brushes are cleaned in the best medium for this purpose—soap and very warm water for acrylic stock, turpentine for oils and lacquer thinner for enamels. Once washed out in any of these, stand the brushes up on the handle end and keep them there until you use them again. This saves money and temper.

Fig. 25–1 Shows the original drawing for the gesso panel which later became the study on which color was used. This drawing is the one traced off on the face of the panel shown in Fig. 25–2.

To illustrate the several steps, I suggest you follow in this part, the problem panel is carved from the design shown in Fig. 25–1. The panel has been turned up on a lathe and is of white pine.

The drawing has been traced off onto the panel. Fig. 25–2

A tracing paper drawing is made on which to work out the color scheme. Fig. 25–1

The panel has been mounted on a back-up and is being bosted out, Fig. 25–3. Note the rather massive rough cuts being made with the grain of the wood. The rim has been completely bosted out and the center back cut to the rim. Fig. 25–4. Be sure you do not let the carving tool come in contact with the raised rim. Be sure the depth of the rim has been developed by back cutting before the bosting out cuts are started.

The figures involved in the design have had the necessary stop cuts made about them prior to bosting out in that area. Fig. 25–4

The rough bosting has been done and the base has been partially stopped off with a broad gouge. Fig. 25–5

The raised figures of the design are now detailed out with suitable tools, a ¼" skew chisel and suitable small gouges are used.

The background and the detailed figures are next sanded off with #120 grit production paper to eliminate some of the coarser tool marks.

Apply gesso, just as it comes from the can to the entire piece, the outside and inside of the rim, the background and the figures. The gesso will take several hours to set up so, be patient.

Examine the gessoed piece for small errors in bosting out, stopping off and modelling. They will exist and are shown up by the gesso. Smooth these places off with the suitable tools—rifflers, gouges, sandpaper or sanding points if necessary. Note: If you use gouges or other edged tools,

Left, Fig. 25–2 Shows the two dolphins traced from the drawing. The first stop cut on the rim has been completed, and back cuts are being made. Right, Fig. 25–3 Bosting out the face of the panel; stop cuts have been made around the dolphins as a safety precaution. Massive cuts have been made by bosting in this operation.

Left, Fig. 25–4 Most of the waste stock has been removed and the dolphins are partially back cut. Note the change on the left-hand dolphin in this illustration. Right, Fig. 25–5 Shows the dolphins nearly profiled out. The next step is to detail them. The background has been stopped off with a broad gouge.

resharpen them before you put them aside. If you use rifflers, clean the gesso from the teeth with the filecard.

The gesso is best applied with a half inch nylon, flat brush or a similar kind. Use this material as it comes from the can.

After the errors and tool marks have been corrected, sand the whole piece off with #150 grit paper. Apply a second coat of gesso. Allow this to dry thoroughly before you attempt to apply any color to the piece of work and when thoroughly dry, lightly repeat the sanding with this fine paper.

This tip may be worthwhile, at least it is a time and trouble saver: Use large pieces of waxed paper on which to put the color stock and you will not have to clean up a pallet or paint can each time you want to do some painting. A little experience will teach you how much abuse the paper can take before you punch holes in it with a bristle brush.

This is where the fun or hard work begins, depending upon your point of view.

I propose to paint this problem panel with acrylic stock and, hopefully, the scheme is this:

The rim, inside and out, a medium yellow.

The background up to the horizon line, deep water blue, but not straight ultra marine blue, however. I will attempt white foam wave crests on the sea.

The sky will shade from a more or less cerulian blue to nearly white on the horizon. I may toss in a couple of clouds, just because.

The porpoises, or bottle nosed dolphins, will be in natural color, gray on top shading off to nearly white on their bellies.

From past experience, I know that there may be need for two, if not three, coats of one of these colors, or more as the case may be; therefore, I will make up enough of each one so that if it becomes necessary to over-paint I won't have to match up the same tones.

I propose to paint the traced off drawing and in so doing, to prevent the tracing paper taking command by wrinkling out of proportion, I will thumbtack down the corners on a piece of plywood.

If the result on the paper pleases my undiscerning eye, I will attempt to duplicate the results on the panel. Fig. 25–6

Fig. 25–6 Shows the color study on which the change in the left-hand dolphin was not made. The left-hand picture is that of the completed dolphins placed along side the study for comparison.

Once this is done, and dry, I will apply a mat finish or varnish made by the same people who make the gesso, the color stock and so on. This will protect the surface from dust and casual abuse.

It well may be that your first endeavor leaves much to be desired. I admit the probability is considerable. However, I submit the idea that for your own benefit you keep the whole thing together, the study and the final results, so when you next make a polychromed panel or carving you can see how much better, or worse, the second and succeeding efforts are than was the first venture.

Further examples of using polychromed finishes for carved panels are shown in Fig. 25–7, a pair of American Widgeons, and Fig. 25–8, a carved panel with rope molding edge which I call "The Eagle and The Sea." Both carvings show the birds in full color; acrylic stock was used on both panels.

Left, Fig. 25–7 The panel is completed. Mastic varnish has been applied as the sealant. Below left, Fig. 25–8 Using the same techniques that were described in the previous illustration and text, this pair of ducks was made. Below right, Fig. 25–9 Photograph of another application of the same techniques called "The Eagle and the Sea." This is one of my favorite pieces.

26
Gilding
a Carving

The term "gilding" always refers to the application of gold or other metallic leaf to a previously prepared surface. Otherwise, the application of imitation gold paint is referred to as gilt or gilting. There is a lot of difference. Not infrequently, some people will use imitation gold leaf, or if you prefer, pinchbeck stock. Look this up in the dictionary!

The term properly "prepared surface" describes the several needed processes that are to be followed before the gold leaf is applied. First, the carving has been done. The details have been developed and the surface has been smoothed down, if that is desired, Fig. 26–1. Next, the surfaces to be gilded have been sized with the proper medium, gesso or the best kind of undercoating available. I prefer aluminum paint applied in three coats for the undercoater on carvings to be used out of doors, otherwise, commercial gesso. Fig. 26–2

In either case, the first coat will show up the inequalities of the work done and these are corrected.

Next, the first coat of sealer-filler is sanded off smoothly.

Two or more, if necessary, coats of the filler or undercoating material must be applied and smoothed off with fine sandpaper.

Next, the piece has to be thoroughly dry and the surface hard.

Then the gilding size has to be applied. This material is a specially prepared stock made by any one of several companies. It is available in three sorts—one, quick set synthetic size; two, slow set colored size; and third, slow set oil size, uncolored. These last two kinds are made from linseed oil that has been allowed to come to the smoking stage in heating. You can, like homemade gesso, make your own but why be that much of a purist if it isn't necessary. You don't have to do everything the hard way.

I use the quickset synthetic size for many of my pieces and this cuts down the waiting time and does an acceptably good job. Color has to be added to this or any other clear size if it is to be used over aluminum paint. The holidays can be seen and size applied to these holidays. Fig. 26–2

It is not necessary to apply color to size if it is to be used on gessoed surfaces but I do so (habit, I suppose).

The size should be applied as evenly as possible and thoroughly brushed smooth in all the deep crevices on the carving to prevent "puddling," that is, accumulating so as to delay the setting of the size.

Before the routine procedure is outlined, a word about gold leaf. It comes in rolls, in mounted leaf and unmounted leaf. It can be either 23 karat, the purest gold, or 22 karat gold, slightly less pure and slightly thicker. I prefer 23 karat gold leaf for my work, the material is more easily

Top, Fig. 26–1 The carved pineapple panel which will be used to illustrate the process of gilding. Center, Fig. 26–2 Half the panel has been colored with the first coat of aluminum paint. Bottom, Fig. 26–3 A second coat of aluminum as a sealer-filler is partially applied.

applied. Mounted leaf consists of leaf that is backed up with thin tissue and is usually used out of doors. Unmounted leaf is a little more difficult to master when you start gilding but the tricks of the trade are readily learned and I suggest this be the kind you use for most of your work. Roll leaf can be applied on some kinds of work but it is not usually used for carvings. There are several makers of gold leaf, both in this country and abroad. German and Italian leaf are quite commonly used here in some places.

The routine procedures for gilding are outlined in the following, presuming the carving has been properly prepared.

Apply the size and let it "gain its tack." Figs. 26–1, 26–2, and 26–3

Place the carving on a bench, preferably on a clean bench cloth for this reason: You can save the fragments that occur when the leaf fractures in its application and use these bits for filling in the skips and holidays that are sure to happen. If portions of the back of the carving are to be gilded, see that the piece is supported clear of the bench cloth.

Be sure you have sufficient gold leaf at hand to complete the work before you size the piece, by the way.

Open the book of gold leaf and hold much in the manner shown in Fig. 26–4. Hold it just over the point at which you are to start gilding. Figs. 26–5, 26–6, and 26–7

Use a sable brush or a gilder's tip, whichever you prefer, and rub the sables in your hair to start a static charge so you can lift the piece of gold leaf from the book and slide it onto the place where the carving has been sized. Fig. 26–8

When the leaf has landed, laid down is the term I use, on the size, brush it out as best you can so it will be smoothed out and spread about that area as completely as possible. Fig. 26–9

Aside from the fact that this lifting, laid on and brushed out series of operations, is seemingly repeated endlessly, that is about all there is to the business.

Of course, it is necessary to go back from time to time to be sure you gild the skipped areas which, as I have said, are bound to occur.

When the entire piece has been gilded, set it aside in a dust-free area and let it stay at least overnight. If you work in an unheated shop in winter,

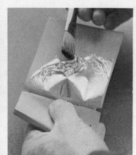

Above from left to right, Fig. 26–4 Color size has been applied over the pineapple, and the first step in the process of gilding is shown. Fig. 26–5, Fig. 26–6, and Fig. 26–7 The three steps required to pick a leaf of gold from a book of unmounted leaf. Left, Fig. 26–8 The gilding operation is nearly completed. This photograph shows how the gold is worked on and into the details of the carving.

Top, Fig. 26–9 The final bits of gold are brushed into and on the carving and the fines are smoothed down. Center, Fig. 26–10 The gilding has been completed. The gold has been brushed, and the final coat of color has been partially applied to the background of the carving. This shows how the color stock eliminates the gilding that always should surround a piece carved in alto relievo as was this. Bottom, Fig. 26–11 The finished panel.

forget trying to gild a carving in the shop. Do it in a heated area instead. Furthermore, do not allow a newly gilded carving to stay in an unheated area during the cold winter months, either. The size will take forever and a day to set.

Once the size is hard, the piece should be burnished.

This may be done in one of three ways, the first with a short bristle sable brush, being sure not to brush too hard on the gold.

It can also be burnished with a piece of real honest-to-god silk velvet, hard now to come by in this synthetic age. If this material is used, do so with care and not too much pressure on the cloth.

If certain areas are to be burnished to a high gloss, use a burnishing agate specially made for this sort of use and again do so lightly, until the gloss is developed. Agate burnishing should never be done on a carving unless gesso has been used as a sealer-filler.

A few tips on this tricky piece of business may not be amiss.

You can determine when the size has "gained its tack" by touching a corner of the sized piece with the skin on the knuckle of your big finger. If the size seems to stick to the skin as you lift your hand and if the size does not come off, actually on the skin, its tack is ready for gilding; otherwise, wait it out.

Be sure the shop is dust free before you size a carving.

Be sure you have a medium width, $1/2''$ or $3/4''$ width, long hair sable brush for gilding. Do not let the hair touch the size, lest it fractures and gets stuck.

If the sheet of gold seems reluctant to be separated from the rouged page of the book, blow gently on one corner of the gold leaf and it will come free. Blow too hard and you lose the piece on the floor.

By folding the rouge paper back on itself as in Fig. 26–4, the gold is more easily separated from the paper.

After all the gilding of the piece seems to be completed, brush the fines, these are the small fragments of broken leaf, back and forth on the carving and you will fill in the very small places where the gold fractured and did not cover over the sized areas. This may render the resizing of the piece and subsequent regilding unnecessary.

If you have some fines, so-called, left over, pour them carefully into a container with a tight cover and save them to brush over the next piece you are to gild. Don't forget, gold is hard money.

One parting though, it may sound or read as if this art of gilding can only be learned after a lot of trial and error. This may be true, but—if you will try this art out on glass first and develop your own techniques in so doing, you will be happier with the business.

The final touch on the carving is to lay in the background color which has been partially done in Fig. 26–10.

In Fig. 26–11, the entire background color has been laid in and the carved panel completed.

Glossary

Art. A generic term used to cover a multitude of endeavors in innumerable creative fields. Briefly—broken down into two fields of artistic (sic) endeavor—"fine arts" and "folk arts."

Back Cutting. 1. To carve a detail at an angle from the face—usually done so that the plane of the cut does not show when the carving is viewed vertically. 2. To carve stock away from the back of a carving blank to fit another surface, as in making a stern transom carving. A. To make diagonal cuts toward the stop cuts to develop a raised detail, as in the development of an eagle's leg.

Band Saw. A power tool that operates an endless steel blade used to cut intricate curves.

Beaking. Molding made with an outwardly rounded portion or section.

Billet. An irregularly shaped piece of wood on which no processes have been undertaken in order to shape it up other than, perhaps having cut it off the end of a thick plank or log.

Billetheads. Elaborately carved finials for the bows of vessels.

Bosting. The first cuts made with carver's tools to reduce the piece to a rough approximation of the desired form, thickness, or section.

Bottoming Off or Stopping Off. Cuts made to finish off the bottom of a hollowed out area. They are carved out to emphasize that section of a carving.

Brads. Small nails or steel pins.

Break the Edge. Sanding or planing off sharp edges to a short radius or curve.

Burnish. To polish to a high luster.

Burr. 1. A roughness on a tool handle. 2. A broken edge or end on an edged tool. 3. The wire, i.e., the thin portion of steel that results from sharpening a tool on coarse stone.

Cartouche. An oval, round, or otherwise shaped design, usually applied on a surface. Sometimes referred to as a cartoon.

Carving Blank. A piece of wood prepared for the purpose of making a carved form there-on by cutting it to approximate length and width and planing off the surfaces of the wood for the reception of the drawing for the carving or portion there-of.

Catheads. Timbers that project beyond the deck and hull of a vessel in the bow for the purpose of lifting the anchor clear of the water.

Chamfer. 1. A sloped or angular surface. 2. A tapered piece. 3. The border of a raised panel.

Checks. In wood, the cracks that occur through improper drying, usually at the ends of planks or billets.

Chisels. Straight, flat tools with various kinds of cutting edges. Straight: cutting edge is at right angles to the long side of the tool. Skew: edges are at an angle of more than 90 degrees to the long side of the tool. Usually a chisel has a single heel; a skew, two heels.

Clamps. Any device used to hol dthe stock in place, either for glueing or on the bench for working.

Clutter. Things saved which, hopefully, will be used again sometime.

Compound Carving. One that is built up of several pieces.

Counterbore. A hole bored into wood with a specially shaped tool bit. Its purpose is to locate the head of a wood screw well below the surface of the surrounding material and to provide a hole in which a plug can be set.

Countersink. A tool made with angular cutting surfaces so that the head of a wood screw can be located slightly below the surface of the surrounding material. The resulting hole is filled with plastic wood or the like.

Cove Molding. Molding made by hollowing out a portion of the stock. From *cavetto* (Latin).

Curl. 1. Swirls or twists in the grain structure of wood. 2. The way a piece of wood will warp.

Cut Off Stop Guide. An appliance used on a sawtable to enable the operator to saw off several pieces all of which are the same length.

Detail Carving. The reduction of the bosted, or rough, carving to the desider shape, profile, or detail. The final step in producing the finished carving.

Dight. The same as a smidgin. A very small quantity.

Dingus. Any kind of a handy piece of equipment that works—usually associated with a handy-billy.

Draw Shave. A steel tool with a long cutting edge and handles set at right angles thereto. Used to reduce edge stock to the desired rough outline or profile.

Driving a Tool. To use a mallet to force the edge of a tool into wood. *Overdrive* means to force the tool into the wood to the point where the cut is too deep and the wood splits or the tool is broken.

Dry Run. A trial run with a piece of stock equal to the parts to be made in which all the processes involved are duplicated.

Dutchman. A tapered oval piece of wood as an inlay in repairing a blemish or miscut in the surface of a carving.

Dyes. Colors prepared from chemicals used to change the appearance of stock. (Personally, I don't like to use dyes.)

Earth Colors. These are finely divided dry colors made from various types of clay or mineral salts or precipitants, usually fired or baked at high heat. These are fast colors, i.e., they never change in color or tone after being exposed to light.

Face Side. That portion of stock that is inside the guide or profile lines and from which the carving is to be made.

Fag-in. To insert or apply a thin piece of stock over a blemish or a tool mark made in error. Making the necessary cuts for this purpose.

False Transom. A mock-up of a real transom for shop use only.

Fascine Binding. The formal adoption of the shape of a binding for a bundle of sticks or faggots.

Fiddleheads. Finials for vessel's bow carved to resemble the head of a fiddle or violin.

Figurehead. A carved design or figure placed on the upper part of a vessel's bow, usually directly below the bowsprit.

Finial. A relatively small, ornamental, terminal detail.

Finish. The method and material used to complete the exterior of a carving and to protect it.

Gesso. A mixture of animal glue, water and whiting: by volume, about 3 parts glue, 5 parts whiting and 12 parts water. To make: Heat water in double boiler, melt glue in it, add whiting. Apply thinly with a brush. Used as a base for fine, bright gilding or for polychrome work. Gesso is now available in commercial form, wet or dry, and is superior to home-made, which is described above.

Gilding. The application of gold leaf to a surface.

Gilding Size. *See* Size.

Gilt. A paint. A poor substitute for gold leaf. Another term for this is "pinchbeck."

Gouges. The carving tools which, in cross-section, are curved to various radii.

Grain. 1. The manner in which the fibers of wood grow. 2. The direction in which the fibres appear to go in a section of wood.

Grit. Size of the crystalline material applied to sandpaper. The higher the number, the finer the size "grit"; applies to grinding wheels and oil-stones as well.

Guide Lines. Lines drawn on the bosted surface of a carving along which the various tools are to be run for finished carving detail.

Hailing Port Board. A specially shaped piece made to fit on a stern transom on which the port of registry of the vessel is carved or incised.

Half Joint. A joint made in one half the thickness of a piece of stock on the end or side so that another piece can be jointed up or glued to the piece, the joints being equal.

Heel. In woodworking tools, that portion of the tool which is on the underside at the cutting edge.

Hold-down. A piece of plywood screwed to the back of a carving blank; used to hold the blank on the bench top.

Hone. A fine-grained sharpening stone. When using a hone, use water or saliva as a lubricant. Wipe stone dry when through sharpening tool.

Hot Glue. Animal glue that must be melted in hot water to use.

Incise, Incised. Carved and modelled areas finished off below the surrounding area or finished face of stock.

Index. 1. To indicate the point where adjacent parts of a drawing are to come together and exactly coincide. 2. To mark.

Interrupted Cut. A cut made on stock with the rotary saw in such a manner that the cut is made within the two ends of the piece, i.e., not made the entire length of the piece.

Jack Plane. A short-bodied hand plane. *See* Planes.

Jigsaw. A power tool that is used to cut curves by means of a short blade moving in an up-and-down motion. Useful for stock that is up to 1 inch in thickness.

Joint. The art of joining two pieces of wood together. Edge jointing, face jointing, tenons and dovetails are all methods of joining.

Kiln Dried. Term describing wood that has been placed in a sealed room and subjected to high, dry heat to remove its moisture.

Lead. The length of the heel of an edged woodworking tool, i.e., a chisel, gouge, plane iron, and so on.

Lining Out. Drawing in the guide lines on a carving.

Long Bend or Bent. A gouge whose blade is formed with a large radius or curve. Also short bend or bent.

Long Lead. A long tapered edge on woodworking tools.

Mill Planed Stock. Stock that has been planed at the lumber mill with rotary planers. These surfaces must always be hand-planed before the stock is either jointed or finished.

Mock-up. A temporary form made to represent, as closely as is possible, a finished surface or object. Used when the original object cannot be at hand on which to fit a carving.

Model. In carving, to develop the final shape of a piece or detail with variously shaped tools. Also, modelling cuts.

Motif. The theme. The salient part of a design or work.

Name Board. Usually similar in shape to the hailing port board when applied to a vessel's stern. Also applied on both sides of a large vessel's bow.

Oiling. Application of raw or boiled linseed oil to the finished carving.

Outline Cuts. Cuts made to outline details.

Overcarve or Overcut. Taking off too much stock when bosting out.

Overlay. Stock that is to be applied to the base of a piece to increase its thickness to the desired plane.

Overrun. To carve the finished detail beyond the guide lines, thus carving away stock that should be left for further detail. A good way to spoil a carving.

Panel Raising. That portion of a panel that projects slightly above the chamfered borders; the surface on which a carving is to be made.

Pare. To take light cuts with hand tools. Usually used when speaking of exterior cuts, as when finishing profiles. To smooth up and finish off the face of stock with light cuts so as to match it up with an adjacent piece.

Parting Tool. A carving tool with a double-edged shaped in the form of a V, the sides being at several different angles in various numbered tools.

Pierced Carving. A carving that uses holes to emphasize some of the detail. Piercings always go all the way through a carving and are made by boring holes, carving holes or sawing holes completely through the stock, as laid out in the design.

Pitch Pocket. Sappy inclusion in pine or any resinous wood that is entirely surrounded by the wood structure.

Planes. 1. The different thicknesses or surfaces of a carving. 2. Hand tools described as follows: Block, 3 to 6 inches long; Fore, 18 inches long; Jack, 14 inches long; Jointer, 21 inches long; Smoother, 9 inches long. The names often identify the uses. "Fore" is for finishing the face and edge, flat.

Plug Cutter. Specially shaped tool for cutting plugs from wood. Plugs are cut across the grain. Dowels are cut with the grain. This tool will make both.

Polychrome. Many-colored.

Polychroming. The application of paints to a carving.

Profile. 1. The lines scribed or drawn outlining the shape of the carving. 2. The actual outline of a carving after it has been cut from the original stock. Also the outline of another form or object.

Rails. The sides of a frame.

Rasp. A coarse-toothed file used especially for wood. It cuts very fast. Smaller, specially shaped rasps are called *rifflers*.

Relief. A special form of carving in which a figure or design is projecting from the general plane of the piece on which it is carved.

Relieve. To cut away stock in order to emphasize the detail.

Reveal. A right angled cut made on one edge of a frame in which a mirror glass or other form of back-up material can be placed.

Rifflers. Specially shaped wood rasps for removing stock from difficult places in the carving. Used in place of edged tools at times.

Rope Molding. A carved section representing the lay of rope. Used mostly for border areas or for contrast with other moldings.

Rounding Off. Process of finishing up surfaces or portions of a carving requiring a rounded exterior. Breaking or rounding the sharp corners on the edges of stock.

Rubbed Back. A term applied when the high gloss of a varnish finish is rubbed over with rottenstone (finely divided pumice) and raw oil to reduce the gloss to a satin-smooth finish.

Run of the Grain. The direction of the grain of the wood.

Running Cuts. Continuous cuts made parallel with the run of the grain of the wood.

Sap Streaks. Imperfections found in resinous woods. Streaks of hardened sap or resin most commonly found in white pine; very infrequently found in mahogany.

Scribe. 1. A pencil compas. 2. To mark a line. 3. To indicate a depth for a sinking.

Scrolls. 1. Shaped boards on which running designs are carved. 2. Running designs carved directly on a portion of the carving.

Scroll Saw. A hand tool used to cut intricate curves; sometimes called a *turning saw* or a *coping saw.*

Seal. To fill the wood structure with a foreign material—white lead, lithopone, or the like—to prevent adsorption of oils or other vehicles used in finishing processes.

Setup. An arrangement of tools or appliances on mechanical tools that is designed to facilitate the production of parts.

Shakes. Separations of the grain of wood longitudinally, usually the result of high winds twisting trees.

Sinking. A deeply depressed area in a carving.

Size. 1. The application of a specially prepared varnish to the surface of a carving for the purpose of providing an adhesive bond for gilding. 2. The commercial varnish so used.

Skew. 1. At an angle. 2. A specially shaped chisel.

Slips. Specially shaped, small sharpening stones.

Spoke Shave. A steel tool with two handles, about 8 inches long overall, used to make finished cuts on vertical surfaces. It is a trickly tool to use.

Stern Transom. The aftermost portion of a vessel's hull, more or less vertical and slightly rounded, which runs from one side of the boat to the other.

Stiles. The top or intermediate or bottom horizontal members of a frame, door or the like.

Stone. Usually this term is applied to a fast-cutting emery or carborundum stone used for sharpening tools.

Stop Cuts. Vertical cuts made about the outline of a portion of a carving. These cuts are made to stop the edge of a tool used in back cutting about a detail so that it will be stopped before it overruns the design or detail.

Strop. A piece of leather loaded with very fine emery powder (#400) used for finish-sharpening edged tools.

Sweeps. Long, continuous cuts made with a gouge in woodcarving.

Tack. In gilding, the stickiness of the gilding size.

Tack Board. An area on a shop wall on which tools of various kinds are hung on nails.

Tang. A tongue or projecting part of a piece used in making a joint in a compound carving or frame.

Template. Usually a thin piece of stock made to fit a surface as exactly as possible from which a duplicate of the original may be made.

Throat of a Cut. The bottom of a finished cut, usually applied to diagonal cuts as in rope moldings.

Tools. Generally divided into two categories: hand tools and machine tools. Hand tools are those that are used in the hand of the operator. All carving and most carpenter's tools are in this category. Machine tools are power-driven mechanical aids only and are used primarily to prepare stock for final manipulation with hand tools.

Trailboards. Carvings made on specially shaped pieces applied on both sides of a vessel's bow.

Transfer. To trace the outline of a drawing on a piece of stock by means of carbon paper placed between the original drawing and the stock, carbon side down preferably.

Transom. A permanent partition on board ship. *See* Stern Transom.

Try piece. A short section of stock, equal in dimension to the material to be finally used, on which trial cuts on the sawtable are made to be sure the setup is correct.

Undercuts. Cuts usually made on the edges of a carving that slope inwardly. Also cuts made on the underside of a carving to fit another piece or object tightly.

Vehicle. The medium or substance in liquid form in which color stock is let down or mixed. It is usually made of linseed oil, turpentine, varnish, japan or dryer mixed together in varying proportions.

Vise. A special device designed to hold work firmly in place between its jaws.

Waste Side. 1. When profiling or cutting out stock for any purpose, the waste side is the part of the board or plank *outside* the drawn guide or profile lines. 2. That portion of the stock that is to be cut off or carved off and thrown away. Also termed "waste stock side."

Web. That portion of stock left when two or more holes are bored adjacent to but not touching each other, as in making a piercing. *See also* Pierced Carving.

Wind. A cut made by a carving tool that is being rotated about its longitudinal axis as the tool is "led through" the wood, that is, as the cut is being made.

Autobiographical Note

The author was born in Melrose, Mass. in 1897. He went to sea as a cadet on the Mass. Nautical Schoolship *Ranger* in 1914. In 1916 he served on the full rigged ship *Timandra*.

In 1917 he was commissioned as Ensign, USNRF and served throughout World War I, going overseas, on U.S.S. *Saranac*.

He married his present wife, Eleanor Russell, in 1920, and their only daughter Sarah was born in 1922. Between the time of his marriage and World War II, his many activities included research, development and inventing with a Cambridge manufacturing company.

Ordered to active duty in April of 1942, he served with the Naval Transportation Service as Convoy Operations and Control Officer in both the Atlantic and Pacific areas. After being invalided stateside in 1944, he was placed on the retired reserve list in 1946.

The Uptons moved to Maine from Wayland, Mass. in 1947 and settled on the shore of Broad Cove in a 1750 farm house.

The author started woodcarving professionally in 1948 after receiving tremendous response to an advertisement placed in a nationally known magazine. The author has continued to receive tremendous response to his woodcarving efforts.

In the past 25 years the author has completed more than 450 carvings, most of which were made to order and sold. In addition to the carvings, he has also constructed many pieces of furniture that were decorated with a wide variety of carvings.

His first book, *The Art of Woodcarving*, was published in 1958.

INDEX

162